Reward and Diversity

Making fair pay add up to business advantage

Sally Brett

First published 2006

Cover design by Curve
Designed by Beacon GDT
Typeset by Paperweight
Printed in Great Britain by Short Run Press, Exeter

British Library Cataloguing in Publication Data
A catalogue record for this book is available from the British Library

ISBN   1 84398 158 0
ISBN-13   978 1 84398 158 9

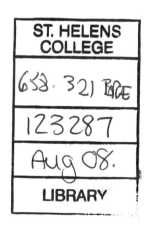
Chartered Institute of Personnel and Development,
151 The Broadway, London SW19 1JQ

Tel: 020 8612 6200
Website: www.cipd.co.uk

Incorporated by Royal Charter. Registered charity no. 1079797.

Contents

Acknowledgements

This executive briefing was researched and written for the CIPD by Sally Brett of Incomes Data Services, with additional research carried out by Sue Milsome. IDS is grateful to all the employers and independent experts who assisted with the research. In particular, we would like to thank the members of the CIPD advisory panel who guided the project – Nicola Allison, Paul Bissell, Charles Cotton, Lynne Fisher, Sue O'Neill, Nic Turner, Caroline Waters, Dianah Worman, and Vicky Wright.

Foreword

The recent focus on the persistent gap between the average earnings of men and women has been stimulated by the campaign, started in the early 1990s by the Equal Opportunities Commission (EOC), to give impetus to the removal of gender pay inequality, as legislation introduced back in the 1970s had failed to achieve this.

Activity began with a task force set up by the EOC in 1999 to explore the views and experiences of a wide range of stakeholders, and was followed by the independent investigation carried out in 2001 by Denise Kingsmill, and a review by the Women and Work Commission chaired by Baroness Prosser, due to report in early 2006.

However, apart from the pressures from the EOC for stronger law, its call for voluntary equal pay reviews as an interim measure to effect progress has been accompanied by a warning that if progress remains stubbornly sluggish, more pressure will be exerted by compulsory interventions. In the meantime, the Commission has published research and guidance and an equal pay review tool to support employers in making changes needed to remove unjustifiable pay anomalies.

The CIPD strongly supported a voluntary approach to pay reviews and worked with the EOC to develop and promote guidance and track progress through surveys. CIPD evidence, published in 2006, showed that just over half of employers surveyed had already completed or planned to complete an equal pay review.

However, even though many employers have been carrying out equal pay reviews, national statistics show that the gap between the average earnings of men and women has not significantly reduced, and at one stage in 2004 it had slightly increased.

So, despite more voluntary activity, the average earnings gap has not narrowed, so it seems implausible that compulsory reviews on their own will work better than voluntary activity. It can be speculated that the outcomes might be even less impressive, because there are many complex and diverse factors contributing to gender pay inequality, some of which are *structural* and informed by societal and personal norms and values regarding *men's* and *women's* jobs and pay and men and women's pay expectations. The latter inform market rates and are, arguably, not totally within the scope of individual employers to address easily.

It is also clear that, where equal pay reviews show unexplainable differences in figures, simply throwing money at the problem will not deliver lasting results, it will only cover up underlying causes which will lead to the same problems in the future. Acting in haste to get a short-term result will waste scarce financial resources and add to the inertia caused by the fear of the cost of removing pay differences.

This fear of unrelenting cost implications prevents employers from taking action, believing that this is one can of worms to be avoided, and some employers may think a better strategy is to sit tight, close their eyes and hope no one will make a claim and, if they do, to just pay them off and keep quiet. This might seem like a good idea but, unfortunately, it is naive and runs the risk of exposure to public recrimination and damaged corporate reputation, with all the cost implications this would incur, not to mention risks regarding harmonious employee relations.

The fear about cost can put employers off carrying out equal pay reviews and encourage them to block change. But direct cost is not the only barrier. We also need to help employers to understand why getting involved in what appears to be an over- whelming bureaucratic exercise of detailed investigation, especially in the absence of good records and helpful technology, in order to find out about underlying causes, makes business sense. This will help to increase the momentum of progress. Simply looking at patterns of figures is not enough to induce systemic change. There has to be a will to find the way, and only guidance and awareness-raising about the benefits will encourage this to happen.

This is where we hope this briefing on reward and diversity will make a difference in organisations – by helping readers to understand that, unless we check that fairness goes beyond gender issues, (which has shown us how important it is to be rigorous), as a key component of reward strategies, we will fail to engage employees' trust and commitment and the discretionary effort they exercise in their jobs. Research evidence proves that discretionary effort is fundamental to improving productivity and performance, so making sure we tap into it is vital to sustaining economic success. Far from being just a *nice* thing to do or *morally* right – treating all people *fairly* is essential to the business case for diversity and good people management and the added value that the workforce can contribute.

If people don't feel valued they become demotivated and disengaged. We know that some service-based, knowledge-intensive firms can spend over 50 per cent of their overheads on pay and reward and that perceptions of unfair pay demotivates people, so there is a financial imperative to make sure reward strategies and interventions reward contribution, not prejudice or bias. Similarly, talented individuals are not going to work for an organisation they believe will not equitably reward and recognise their performance. Scrutinising their worth through regular equal pay reviews, using various diversity dimensions will help to build quality into reward systems and processes and ensure that pay relativities are deemed fair and acceptable.

As Lord Layard explains in his book *Happiness*[1], if we don't get enough money we feel unhappy but, beyond a certain point we are more concerned with pay relativities with others, and if these are not felt to be fair we become dissatisfied. Dissatisfied employees don't make a good workforce, so reward strategies and interventions clearly need to engage feelings of fairness and worth in order to be successful.

We need to make sure they do this by interrelating diversity issues and total reward strategies. A marriage of both disciplines will help organisations to create the workplace environment demanded by today's sophisticated workforce and competitive markets.

This briefing is aimed at diversity and reward specialists to help them work together with personnel practitioners by bringing their perspectives together in ways that will bring about the changes organisations need to make to ensure reward for work is fair.

Dianah Worman
Adviser, Diversity
Chartered Institute of Personnel and Development

Charles Cotton
Adviser, Reward
Chartered Institute of Personnel and Development

Endnote

1   LAYARD R. *Happiness: lessons from a new science*. New York: Penguin Press, 2005

Executive summary

In the last five years, a great deal of attention has been focused on the persistence of the gender pay gap in the UK. Numerous research projects and investigations have been carried out to try and establish what lies behind it (the latest being the Women and Work Commission) and multiple recommendations have been made. For employers, the pressure has been on for them to carry out equal pay reviews and to prove that they are not discriminating against women in their reward systems and practices.

This renewed focus on equal pay has brought reward and diversity professionals into much closer contact with each other – indeed, for many organisations an equal pay review has been the first equality-related initiative in the reward arena. But, rather than use it as an opportunity to consider wider issues, such as ensuring equity in reward and recognising the growing diversity of the workforce through reward, it has often led to a narrow and overly legal view of the reward and diversity relationship. Where equal pay reviews have been carried out, they have often led to long discussions about the reliability of the data and whether or not any gender pay inequalities uncovered by the review are justifiable under the Equal Pay Act (equal pay claims are rarely straightforward).

Nevertheless, in a few organisations, the issue of equal pay has been addressed within a broader context. Equal pay reviews and subsequent actions have been driven, not by what the Equal Pay Act says, but by a commitment to the values of equity and inclusion, and a recognition that effective employee engagement depends upon ensuring all individuals, regardless not just of gender but of any irrelevant non-job related criteria, are fairly rewarded for their efforts.

Such an approach makes more sense than the narrowly legal one, given the growing diversity of the workforce and the importance of an organisation's people, and its ability to engage them, in creating competitive advantage. After all, the gender pay gap has become a hot topic again not because of recent legal developments – the Equal Pay Act has been in place for 30 years. It has become an issue because of what it represents – the under-utilisation of the skills and talents of a significant and valuable part of the workforce.

In this executive briefing, we explore the wider interaction between reward and diversity. We intend to provide reward and diversity specialists with a greater understanding of each other's disciplines and to give them, and those with a more general HR focus, a clearer idea of the potential overlap between the two.

Key points

◘ *Reward and diversity*

Expectations of both the reward and diversity functions have shifted in the past decade to become more strategic and supportive of business goals. Both seek to engage employees and central to this is ensuring individuals receive a fair reward for their work. The growing diversity of the workforce needs to be considered when designing reward strategies.

◘ *What is fair reward?*

Fair reward means providing equal pay in all instances of equal work, unless there is an objectively justifiable business-related reason for varying pay and benefits. Fair reward employers have fair and objective criteria for determining reward, fair and objective reward processes, and regularly monitor reward decisions to check for any bias or inequity.

◘ *Equal pay reviews*

Equal pay reviews are a good starting point for addressing fair reward as they identify the current reward distribution and where the main inequities lie. Reviews should look at how fairly all individuals are treated and whether or not the reward strategy is being effectively

implemented. They should not focus solely on assessing the risk of equal pay claims and minimising legal costs.

◘ *Fair reward practice*

Fair reward practice means ensuring objectivity in all aspects of reward. A rational and objective approach to managing pay relativities (such as analytical job evaluation) should underpin grading structures and pay progression should realistically reflect the time it takes a satisfactory performer to become fully competent and effective in post. Variations in pay and benefits for those doing equal work may be justified if they are a proportionate means of achieving a legitimate business end. If reward decisions are devolved to line managers they must understand why diversity is important to the organisation, and they should be given the skills necessary for them to implement reward in a fair and non-discriminatory way and their decisions need to be regularly monitored and reviewed.

◘ *Reward communications*

To realise the full benefits of a fair reward approach on employee engagement and motivation, organisations must provide clear and effective communications on reward principles, reward processes, and the actions taken to ensure objectivity and alignment with strategic business goals. Listening to employees

and seeking their opinions on reward can
provide valuable information on how reward is
working in practice.

◘ *Diversity through reward*

Reward packages can be designed to attract a
more diverse workforce and incorporating
diversity goals or competencies into a
contribution-related pay system can help create
a culture that is supportive of diversity. Flexible
benefits and total reward strategies are suited
to organisations that recognise individual
diversity.

◘ *Key recommendations for action*

Organisations can structure their approach to
reward and diversity and plan actions to make
reward fairer and more responsive to a diverse
workforce by working through the list of key
recommendations.

- Reward and diversity have both become more strategic and focused on the individual employee

- Employee engagement depends upon rewarding individuals fairly, in practice, not just in theory

- The growing diversity of the workforce needs to be considered when designing and implementing reward strategies

1 | Introduction

Expectations of both the reward and diversity functions have changed in the last decade. Reward used to be about the effective administration of compensation and benefits structures, while diversity, or equal opportunities as it was more commonly called, tended to focus on ensuring compliance with anti-discrimination laws and specific initiatives for minority groups. However, in recent years, both functions have begun to see a re-interpretation of their roles, from passive administration and compliance, to actively shaping and supporting the delivery of strategic business goals. This shift reflects the wider trend towards 'human capital' management – the recognition that people and how they are managed are fast becoming the key determinants of business success.

In this chapter, we look at recent trends in the development of both the reward and diversity functions and consider the overlap between the two disciplines and the common goals both are trying to achieve. In particular, we highlight the importance of the concept of fairness to the achievement of those goals.

Reward

The main objective of reward used to be to recruit and retain staff while providing a degree of cost control. But in recent years, organisations have taken a more strategic approach to reward and have designed reward systems with multiple objectives in mind. Typically, these include attracting key talent to the organisation, motivating employees to contribute their best, getting employees focused on business goals, and encouraging behaviour compatible with corporate values.

> *'…[reward and diversity] have begun to see a re-interpretation of their roles, from passive administration and compliance, to actively shaping and supporting the delivery of strategic business goals.'*

As Duncan Brown explains in *Reward Strategies*:

Reward systems become an important means of communicating and reinforcing the business goals of the organisation, not just because pay represents an important cost for many organisations, but because reward systems can

Reward and diversity

Traditionally, reward and diversity have had little in common, apart from ensuring compliance with the equal pay legislation, as one appeared to be driven by the demands of the market and financial constraints and the other by the law and moral concerns. However, as the focus of both functions has shifted to place much greater emphasis on recognising employees as individuals, and the aim of both has become to engage employees and to motivate them to work to the best of their capabilities, it is time for a more holistic approach to emerge.

Fair reward

Central to such an approach is the concept of fair reward. Employee engagement depends, not just on the salary and benefits an individual receives, but on whether or not they feel they and their colleagues are being fairly rewarded for their particular skills, knowledge and contribution. People may be motivated to go to work for the money, but their choice of which organisation to work for, and their level of contribution once there, will be influenced, not just by the amount they receive but by whether they feel fairly treated. Professor David Guest[5], in his model of the

Table 1 | Reward strategy objectives *(Source:* CIPD Reward Management Survey 2005*)*

	% of respondents citing as important goal
Support business goals	79
Reward high performers	64
Recruit and retain high performers	62
Link pay to the external market	53
Achieve/maintain market competitiveness	51
Manage pay costs	50
Ensure internal equity	41
Adopted (or adopting) total reward approach	28

psychological contract, has stressed the central importance of fairness and trust in increasing employee commitment, satisfaction and productivity. But few seem to have fully understood the impact fair reward can have on business performance – just 41 per cent of organisations responding to the CIPD annual reward management survey in 2005 mentioned ensuring internal equity as an objective of their reward strategy (see Table 1 opposite).

Most effort, in recent years, appears to have been put into the design of reward systems – building in the mechanisms needed to give greater flexibility and to align reward with strategic business goals. Less time and resources have been devoted to ensuring the effective implementation of reward systems and to evaluating the impact of reward on employees. This is despite the fact that various case-study research has shown that getting the desired response from employees often depends less on the particular set of reward policies and mechanisms adopted, and more on how employees' experience the reward structure and processes. Reward managers need to recognise that unless the reward system is fair, not only in its design, but in its processes and in its outcomes, and is perceived to be fair by employees, their ultimate objective of securing employee engagement and commitment through reward will not be met.

Similarly on the diversity side, the adoption of wide-ranging diversity strategies and the senior level commitment to the values of equity and inclusion will not achieve anything if employees do not see evidence of that commitment in their day-to-day experiences within the organisation, particularly in one of the most fundamental parts of the employment relationship – reward. Those responsible for managing diversity within organisations should not, therefore, shy away from looking at the difficult and sensitive subject of pay, as many previously have. As Fiona Cannon, Lloyds TSB's, head of diversity noted:

Having done such a lot on diversity and equality over the years, it really struck us that without equal pay we wouldn't have achieved anything. Pay is the thing that really does have an impact on people's lives long term as it affects other benefits too, so we felt in order to fulfil our holistic approach to diversity, equal pay had to be a foundation stone. [6]

> **'...getting the desired response from employees...depends less on the...reward policies and mechanisms adopted, and more on how [they] experience the reward structure and processes.'**

Diversity through reward

Finally, when designing and implementing employee-oriented reward strategies, organisations must consider the growing diversity of the workforce. If an organisation's reward objectives include attracting and retaining key talent, then it needs to ensure that the package it is offering appeals to the diverse range of talent that is out there, and that it is not unconsciously limiting itself to a single talent pool because of the way it has designed its pay and benefits structure.

Similarly, if the reward system has been designed to encourage certain kinds of behaviour or provide incentives towards certain goals, then there should be checks to ensure that those behaviours and actions are compatible with its diversity strategy. It may be worth including diversity targets or competencies to show that diversity goals are as important as the other business outputs and behaviours that are being measured and rewarded.

Endnotes

1   BROWN D. *Reward Strategies: From intent to impact*. London: CIPD, 2001.

2   CIPD. *Managing diversity: linking theory and practice to business performance.* CIPD Change Agenda. London: CIPD, 2005.

3   KANDOLA R. and FULLERTON J. *Diversity in Action: Managing the mosaic*. 2nd Edition. London: CIPD, 1998.

4   CIPD. *Managing diversity: people make the difference at work – but everyone is different*. CIPD Guide. CIPD: 2005.

5   GUEST D. E. and CONWAY, N. *Pressure at work and the psychological contract*. London: CIPD, 2002.

6   IDS. 'Tackling equal pay at Lloyds TSB'. *IDS Diversity at Work*. No.14, August 2005. pp.8–12.

- Fair reward means treating people in an objective and equitable way

- It means providing equal pay in all instances of equal work, unless there is an objectively justifiable business-related reason for varying pay and benefits

- To be a fair reward employer, organisations need to adopt fair and objective criteria for determining reward; to ensure reward processes are designed and implemented in a fair and objective way; and to monitor reward outcomes to check for any bias

2 | What is fair reward?

What constitutes fair reward can be a highly subjective and contentious issue, which is perhaps why many organisations – although they may issue broad statements about staff being fairly rewarded for their efforts – tend to avoid openly addressing and communicating on the issue and may not have even considered what they mean by fair reward.

However, as diversity strategies stress the importance of treating individuals in an objective and equitable manner, fair reward, from a diversity perspective, means rewarding individuals according to objective criteria that are relevant to, and help the organisation achieve, its legitimate business aims. Irrelevant non-job-related factors such as an employee's age, sex, ethnicity, disability, sexual orientation, religion or belief, working hours arrangements, marital status, etc, should not have any impact on an individual's pay and benefits, both in theory and in practice. Looked at another way, fair reward means applying the principles of equal pay to the entire workforce and not just to male–female comparisons.

Fair reward principles
Equal pay for equal work

The starting point of any efforts to implement fair reward should begin with the principle of equal

pay for equal work. The Equal Pay Act 1970, as amended by the Equal Pay (Amendment) Regulations 1983, defines equal pay for equal work as providing the same pay to those who are doing:

◘ like work (ie the same or a similar job)

◘ work that is rated as equivalent by an analytical job evaluation scheme

◘ work that may be different but is deemed to be of equal value in terms of factors such as skill, effort and responsibility.

The Equal Pay Act entitles a woman (or man) to the same contractual pay and benefits as a man (or woman) who is doing equal work to them, unless there is a genuine material factor unrelated to the sex of the individuals which genuinely explains that difference. If an organisation is taking a more holistic approach to reward and diversity, the principle of equal pay for equal work needs to be applied to all instances of equal work, and not just to those where a woman is doing equal work with a man, and vice versa.

In fact, many individuals appear to assume that the Equal Pay Act is about providing *fair* pay for everyone, rather than about tackling sex discrimination in reward. In its evidence to the Women and Work Commission, Acas explained that many of the calls from employees to its helpline on the subject of equal pay were actually from men seeking pay equality with other men doing equal work and that workplace advisers also report similar misunderstandings by trade union stewards who interpret equal pay as fair pay, again often comparing pay and conditions between two men.[1]

> *'...many...assume that the Equal Pay Act is about providing fair pay...rather than about tackling sex discrimination in reward.'*

Justifiability of pay variations

The Equal Pay Act allows for variations in pay for men and women doing equal work so long as those variations are due to a genuine and material factor that is unrelated to their sex. The Act does not set out what constitutes a genuine and material factor. An employer would have to present it, if it existed, as a defence to an equal pay claim and it would be up to the tribunal to decide.

As well as showing that the factor giving rise to pay differentials is genuine and material – ie that it is causally relevant and truly explains the difference in pay between the man and the woman – the employer would have to show:

◘ it existed at the time the pay and benefits were set and it continues to exist

◘ it is untainted by direct discrimination

◘ if it is tainted by indirect discrimination (ie it has a disproportionately negative impact on one sex over another) that it is objectively justifiable.

For an indirectly discriminatory factor to be objectively justifiable, the organisation would need to show that varying pay for that reason was necessary to meet real business aims, that it did in fact lead to those aims being met, and that there was no less discriminatory way for the organisation to achieve them.

As many organisations have attempted to more closely align reward to their business strategy and have sought greater flexibility in how reward is determined, many have begun to vary pay and benefits according to factors such as individual performance or competence, or to movements in the external market. Some believe such variations are at odds with equal pay and fair reward, as they lead to deviations from the principle of equal pay for equal work. However, such variations can be consistent with a fair reward approach, so long as it can be shown that:

◘ the criteria for varying pay and benefits are objective and relevant

◘ the variations that occur are actually according to the set criteria

◘ all individuals are treated fairly by the processes determining those variations

◘ the variations lead to legitimate business objectives being met and there is no less discriminatory way of achieving them.

Implementing fair reward

Having outlined, the principles of fair reward above, the four basic elements to implementing fair reward are:

◘ having a clear commitment to fair reward and being clear and transparent about the organisation's reward principles and aims (ie whether or not variations in reward will occur, the criteria by which they will occur, and why they are necessary to further business aims)

◘ having fair and objective processes for determining reward and ensuring that those implementing the reward processes behave in a fair and objective manner

◘ monitoring of reward outcomes to ensure that the reward system and processes are having the desired effect and are not resulting in potentially discriminatory consequences

◘ good communication with employees so that the system and measures implemented are clearly understood and perceived as being fair.

Endnote

1 ACAS. *Evidence to Women and Work Commission.* London: Acas, 2005.

- Equal pay reviews are a good starting point for fair reward as they identify the current reward distribution and where the main inequities lie

- Reviews should look at how fairly all individuals are treated and whether or not the reward strategy is being effectively implemented and should not focus solely on assessing the risk of equal pay claims and minimising legal costs

- Many organisations have encountered difficulties in doing equal pay reviews, but these need to be overcome by better monitoring both of reward decisions and workforce diversity

3 | Equal pay reviews

Equal pay reviews are a good starting point for any attempt to address fair reward as they establish what the current reward distribution is and what the pattern of any inequities might be. The summary figures provide organisations with a snapshot of how reward is distributed and the opportunity to examine whether or not pay gaps between those doing equal work are justifiable – not only from the perspective of compliance with the Equal Pay Act, but also in terms of whether or not the variations that have occurred are according to the criteria set out in its reward strategy and whether or not they fit with its commitment to diversity. Such examinations require delving for the stories behind the figures – not just number crunching.

In this chapter we look at what equal pay reviews involve, organisations' experiences of doing them and the barriers that many have faced in trying to conduct them. We highlight how those organisations that have taken a broader fair reward approach, rather than just checked for compliance with the Equal Pay Act, have carried out their reviews and acted upon the insights that they have gained.

Pressure to do equal pay reviews
EOC Equal Pay Task Force

Equal pay reviews hit most employers' radar screens in 2001 when the EOC's Equal Pay Taskforce[1] recommended that organisations should be required by law to carry them out. The Task Force was surprised by the degree of complacency among employers. It stated that:

We have been struck by the paradox of large numbers of employers giving evidence to the Task Force in which they state with confidence that they do not have a gender pay gap in their organisation. Yet they have not carried out an equal pay review. It has become clear to us that the overwhelming majority of employers think there is no gender pay gap in their organisation but have no evidence to support this belief.

Kingsmill Review

A Government-sponsored investigation into women's pay and employment, which was carried out after the Task Force made its recommendations in 2001, supported the call for employers to review their pay systems, albeit on a voluntary basis. Denise Kingsmill, who chaired the investigation, shared the concerns the Task Force had raised about the lack of information and knowledge organisations appeared to have about the impact of their reward systems in practice. However, it was not compliance with the Equal Pay Act that was of primary concern to her, but the failure of organisations to learn more about what lay behind pay differentials and their failure to realise the business benefits of fully valuing and developing female talent.

Kingsmill[2] called for equal pay reviews to be not just about tackling instances of illegal pay discrimination but about investigating and reporting on how well the organisation was using its human capital. Although she welcomed the development of guidance on how to do equal pay reviews (which the EOC and others were producing), she thought that there was a danger, if the process became too prescriptive and reviews mandatory, that they would become merely tick-box compliance exercises. She explained:

I do not see such reviews as ends in themselves, but rather as essential management tools to enable organisations to identify the challenges they face and to assess the impact of the policies and initiatives they introduce.

She went on:

The experience of companies that I have consulted indicates that employment and pay reviews are most effective in uncovering the strategic

information that will be of benefit to the company as well as its employees when they are driven by business incentives and tied to corporate objectives. The path that the review will take depends upon the specific circumstances of the company involved.

Extent of equal pay review activity

Nearly five years have passed since the EOC's Equal Pay Task Force and the Kingsmill Review made their recommendations and, despite the campaigning and the guidance and assistance that has been made available from the EOC, CIPD, Acas and others, the take-up rate by employers has remained disappointingly low. The latest EOC survey[3] monitoring the extent of equal pay review activity conducted at the end of 2004, found that two-thirds of employers (68 per cent) have not carried out, and have no intention of carrying out, an equal pay review. The CIPD research evidence published in 2005 showed that 50 per cent of employers had carried out an equal pay review.[4]

Reasons for not doing reviews

The most common reason given by organisations for not doing an equal pay review is the belief that they already provide equal pay – 87 per cent of those who had no plans to do a review cited this as the reason in the latest survey conducted for the EOC, reaffirming the findings of the Equal Pay Taskforce. Again, this reflects the complacency that, just because separate male and female pay scales no longer exist and reward is said to vary by non-gender-specific criteria, such as performance or competence, there is no discrimination in pay. But, as we will illustrate in Chapter 4, different reward structures and processes, however non-discriminatory they appear in their design, can have unintended discriminatory consequences and may not be rewarding the factors that were intended to be rewarded, particularly if they are not properly implemented and monitored.

Another reason behind organisations' reluctance to do equal pay reviews is the fear of what might be uncovered. In fact, some employers have turned the minimising legal risk argument put forward for doing equal pay reviews on its head, arguing that if they do one, they may end up highlighting potential legal claims, of which employees were previously unaware. Their fears are compounded by the fact that the Equal Pay Act requires immediate rectification of any inequalities that are found. So, as Acas has said:

Although the moral case for equal pay is widely accepted, the economic argument tends to win out. Many employers, therefore, prefer to take their chances rather than open up a Pandora's box of equal pay.[5]

The EOC, to try and allay employers' fears of what a review might uncover and how much it may cost them to put right, has recently called for equal pay legislation to be amended, so that employers who have done an equal pay review are given a period of amnesty from equal pay claims to close any gaps that are uncovered.

EOC's current position on equal pay reviews

In July 2005, the EOC called for a radical rethink of equality laws, including a new duty on employers to take action on all causes of the pay gap. This duty would require employers to carry out diagnostic 'equality checks' which would look at what action was needed to narrow any gender pay gaps – for those doing equal work, but also any pay gaps that existed across the organisation because of women being concentrated in particular kinds of jobs or at lower levels.

If the equality check found that an organisation was at risk of breaching the Equal Pay Act, then it would be required by law to undertake a full equal pay review. For these employers, the EOC would like the equal pay legislation to be changed to give them an amnesty period from potential claims from individuals to allow them to address the issue.

Jenny Watson, acting chair of the EOC said:

Thirty years on, it's clear the Equal Pay Act has reached the end of its usefulness. The pay gap is simply not closing. It has been stuck at 40 per cent for women working part-time for the past 25 years. Failing to act to reform the law is no longer an option. Without action, Britain's women will continue to be condemned to the indignity and injustice of unequal pay, and employers will bear the risk of costly tribunal cases for a generation to come. It's time to share the responsibility for tackling equal pay more widely… The duty which we are proposing today gives [business] an incentive to [act] through the inclusion of a protected period, or pay amnesty. It has the potential to make best practice common practice and to ensure that all employers can fully benefit from women's skills and talents.

Motivations for doing a review

Organisations that have a narrow view of the interaction between reward and diversity, and see it as primarily being about complying with the Equal Pay Act, are those that will be most concerned with avoiding the costs of losing a legal case. Such organisations may judge it unwise to carry out an equal pay review or, if they do one, they may choose to do it behind closed doors, and are likely to tackle only the most clearly unjustifiable inequalities that are uncovered.

> *'...equal pay reviews are an important starting point and a good benchmark for evaluating future progress on reward and diversity...'*

By contrast, organisations that view reward and diversity from a more holistic perspective will be seeking to avoid the less tangible, but potentially greater, financial loss that comes from having a disengaged and under-utilised workforce. The motivation for such organisations in doing equal pay reviews is to find out how fair and effective their reward systems are in practice. They are more likely to take subsequent action, not just to correct potential equal pay claims, but to improve the effectiveness of reward and to ensure that it is fairer for everyone.

The latter approach is more likely to lead to equal pay reviews being viewed as the 'essential management tools' for improving human capital management that Denise Kingsmill envisaged them being, rather than just becoming 'ends in themselves'.

Equal pay reviews in practice

Interviews and discussions with those that have carried out equal pay reviews in the past five years reveal that most organisations have encountered difficulties in trying to conduct them, usually because of data limitations or difficulties in establishing where men and women are doing equal work across the organisation. Most organisations have, therefore, not been able to carry out the full and thorough analysis recommended by the EOC, at least, not at the first attempt.

However, those organisations who are committed to ensuring fairness in reward have understood that equal pay reviews are an important starting point and a good benchmark for evaluating future progress on reward and diversity, and they have not been deterred by the obstacles they have encountered. Instead, they have tried to set up the information systems necessary to carry out reliable analyses and have sought to improve the process year-on-year, often widening the scope of the review in subsequent years to cover other diversity dimensions such as ethnicity, age and disability.

Recent case-study research carried out by the Institute of Employment Studies (IES)[6] on behalf of the EOC shows that:

◘ the majority of equal pay reviews fail to follow all the steps set out in the EOC's toolkit and are limited in scope

◘ equal pay reviews took the equivalent of three to six months of a single member of staff's time

◘ some organisations complained that it was a lengthy and frustrating process with no clear benefits.

The research also found that, in general, there was no direct link between the time taken to do an equal pay review and the perceived benefits of doing one. (However, the organisation that took the longest amount of time and did the most thorough analysis, was the most positive about the experience.) Furthermore, there was little correlation between the size of the pay gaps found and the likelihood that the organisation would take action subsequent to the review. Some organisations with no gaps or small gaps took action to further reduce the risk of discrimination and make reward fairer, while some of those that found significant pay gaps took no action at all, believing that despite the gaps, the risk of encountering an equal pay claim was manageable. This again highlights the fact that an organisation's motivation for doing an equal pay review shapes the process and the utility of the findings. Where gaps relate to occupational segregation, organisations should consider widening the recruitment base to encourage diversity. For instance, Schneider Electric works with local schools to encourage more girls to go into scientific and technical roles. This is the kind of activity that the initiative Women into Science and Engineering (WISE) promotes.

Tackling job segregation

In France, PSA Peugeot Citröen and Schneider Electric have both recently launched diversity initiatives. PSA Peugeot Citröen's initiatives include significantly reducing the number of jobs in which it is necessary to lift more than 8kg and encouraging more women to opt for scientific and technical studies. In the first year of the programme, they increased the number of women employees by 10 per cent. At the executive level, the company now employs 88 per cent more women.

Schneider Electric has launched a number of plans including:

◘ Women to be trained for jobs in areas that are presently male dominated.

◘ Within five years, salary differences between male and female employees will be less than 1 per cent.

◘ The company will help schools to give better careers education information to girls.

◘ Maternity leave will not adversely influence salary progression.

◘ Training for company employees will now be on site wherever possible so as to reduce travelling.

The equal pay review process

Numerous organisations are now providing guidance and advice on how to carry out equal pay reviews. However, most of these are based on the five-step process described in the EOC's Equal Pay Review Kit outlined below.

> *'...wherever possible an equal pay review should be extended to cover not just gender but other dimensions, such as ethnicity, disability and age...'*

The five-step process is, as follows:

1   Decide the scope of the review and identify the data required.

2   Identify where men and women are doing equal work.

3   Collect pay data to identify gaps between those doing equal work.

4   Establish the causes of the pay gaps and decide whether or not they are free from discrimination.

5   Develop an equal pay action plan to tackle any gaps that can not be explained on grounds other than sex.

The Equal Pay Review Kit stresses that:

An equal pay review is not simply a data collection exercise. It entails a commitment to put right gender pay inequalities and this means that the review must have the involvement and support of managers with the authority to deliver the necessary changes.

The scope of the review

The EOC toolkit recommends that to ensure there are no equal pay liabilities, a review should be company-wide, involving comparisons of pay in all instances where men and women are doing equal work across the organisation. The information needed to do a thorough review includes data on all the elements of reward and information about employee characteristics such as their position in the grading structure, working time arrangements, and length of service.

It suggests that wherever possible an equal pay review should be extended to cover not just gender but other dimensions, such as ethnicity, disability and age, as well. It is sometimes forgotten that pay discrimination claims can be brought under other discrimination laws and not just the Equal Pay Act. Public sector employers who are covered by the public duty to promote race equality, and will soon be covered by a public duty to promote disability equality from December 2006, should at least aim to include analysis of pay by ethnicity and disability within their equal pay reviews. But, ideally, any employer that is committed to the broader principles of diversity and fairness in reward should be concerned to check that there is no bias in their reward systems, not just by sex, but by other factors, such as ethnicity, disability, age, religion or belief, sexual orientation, or working hours status.

But many organisations have found that, despite their good intentions, there is a considerable gap between what they would like to review and analyse within their equal pay review and what they are able to, because they lack all the necessary data on reward and the diversity of their workforce. The limited amount of information organisations currently hold on reward implementation, and the difficulties many have had in tying it up with diversity data, again reflects the general lack of concern there has been up to now about ensuring equity in reward. The IES case-study research found that, in almost all the organisations it looked at, an equal pay review was the first equality initiative aimed specifically at pay issues.

Given that many organisations are likely to be starting an equal pay review without all the necessary data and, in many instances, without knowing what data is required and where it is held, it is likely that the first equal pay review will be limited to an analysis by gender. In addition, some have found it worthwhile to begin their analysis with a smaller pilot review of a particular group of employees or a business division so that they can familiarise themselves with the process, the information that is needed, and the best method for extracting and manipulating it. Where such pilot reviews have been carried out they have alerted the organisation to the biggest problem

areas or risks that a wider analysis is likely to reveal, and have thus allowed them to establish clear priorities for further investigation and to initially target resources at specific initiatives.

Some large organisations have continued with the segmented, business-unit-by-business-unit approach when they have rolled out the equal pay review across the organisation. This is because they have found it to be a beneficial way of getting local managers involved in the process and getting them to take responsibility for the findings and actions to ensure fair reward in their areas. However, it should be borne in mind that limiting the scope of the review and segmenting the process in this way will not ensure compliance with the Equal Pay Act, as equal pay claims can be brought by individuals naming comparators doing equal work in any part of the organisation. So, although it may assist with getting diversity onto the reward agenda with local managers, to ensure full legal compliance, an organisation-wide review would have to be carried out as well.

Reward and diversity project team

It is recommended that an equal pay review be carried out by a project team with a breadth of experience and influence in the organisation. Having a member of staff from reward involved, particularly if they have some history in the organisation and knowledge of how the reward system has evolved over the years, will greatly assist with the understanding of how gaps between individuals could have arisen. Similarly, staff responsible for diversity will help in assessing whether or not differences in pay are deemed to be justifiable from a legal and an equity perspective. They will also be able to shed light and recommend action on other issues that the review reveals, such as the concentration of women or ethnic minorities in particular kinds of jobs, or the lack of diversity in higher job grades or pay bands.

The IES research found that, although most equal pay reviews were carried out or managed by reward staff, where both reward and diversity staff were involved, the reviews tended to be more comprehensive in their analysis and to lead to more wide-ranging actions based on their findings.

Identifying equal work

Once the scope of the review has been determined, the next stage is to establish where individuals are doing equal work. Without an analytical job-evaluation scheme in place covering the whole workforce, this will be a difficult exercise and the reliability of any equal work comparisons that are made in the absence of such a scheme will be questionable. Furthermore, as analytical job evaluation is the most objective method for assessing where equal work is being performed, if an organisation is committed to fairness in reward, whatever grading structure is introduced, it should be underpinned by such a scheme. Only in the case of small employers may analytical job evaluation not be appropriate and the EOC has developed separate guidance for small businesses[7] on how such organisations can establish where equal work is being done in a rational and objective way.

Comparisons of pay within grades or pay bands, even when the structure is not underpinned by an appropriate job evaluation scheme, can still be a useful alert to any inequities in areas such as progression or starting salaries. In addition, the EOC toolkit provides guidance on some alternative ways of establishing where individuals are doing equal work for the purpose of doing an equal pay review. For example, it suggests comparing jobs requiring similar qualification levels or comparing jobs with similar job titles like 'manager' or 'team leader' in different departments. But again, it should be remembered that none of these methods are an adequate substitute for analytical job evaluation and such an equal pay review would not assist in defending a claim based on equal pay for work of equal value at a tribunal.

Even where analytical job evaluation is in place the equal pay review process should include an analysis of whether or not the design of the scheme is equality-proof and whether or not it is being implemented in a fair and non-discriminatory way. This means considering issues such as:

◘ whether or not factors relevant to all jobs were considered in the design of the scheme

◘ whether evaluators are fully trained in equality issues

◘ whether evaluation panels are representative of the workforce

◘ what opportunities there are for jobs to be re-evaluated if they have grown in size

◘ whether or not the applications for, and results of, re-evaluations are monitored by sex, ethnicity, disability etc.

Pay analysis

When it comes to comparing the different elements of pay and benefits of those doing equal work in the third step of the review, a good starting point is to calculate and compare averages – average basic pay, average total pay, average bonus payments, average allowances, etc – as averages give an initial feel for any inequalities. However, it should be remembered that averages hide a lot of detail, so further comparisons need to be carried out as well.

Comparing median pay and benefit levels for different groups gives a more realistic picture of what is happening for the majority of employees, as they strip out the extreme values that can drag averages up or down. Looking at the pattern of distribution for each element of reward will highlight individual anomalies, which may cause concern and warrant further investigation.

When BT carried out its first equal pay review it chose to focus its initial investigations and actions on those individuals whom the analysis of salary distributions revealed were clustered at the lower end of its broad pay bands. It tried to establish whether or not there were justifiable reasons for these individuals earning significantly below the average for their job roles, such as lack of experience or poor performance and, if no such reason existed, the individuals received additional pay awards, whether they were men or women, to progress them more quickly through the pay band.

'Comparing median pay and benefit levels for different groups gives a more realistic picture of what is happening for the majority of employees...'

Extending pay analysis beyond gender

It is particularly difficult to draw meaningful conclusions from averages when doing comparisons by other diversity dimensions, such as ethnicity or disability, where there are often very small sample sizes for some groups. Some organisations have tried to overcome this difficulty by rolling up data for different groups to provide larger sample sizes, so, for example, rather than doing comparisons for separate minority ethnic groups, the average pay and benefits of all non-white employees would be compared to that of all white employees. The drawback of such an approach is that the problems faced by particular minority groups can become obscured within the larger sample.

A more detailed form of analysis would be to carry out comparisons of matched samples, as Nationwide Building Society has tried to do since it has extended its equal pay review to include ethnicity as well. This means comparing the pay of individuals from each minority group with the pay of individuals from the majority group with similar characteristics to them, such as similar length of service, qualifications and employment history. Although identifying the comparators takes more time and can be more resource intensive than just rolling up the data, it provides a more accurate picture and a more reliable basis on which to plan and take action to correct any specific patterns of discrimination.

Establishing causes of pay gaps

Once gaps in the pay and benefits of those doing equal work have been identified, the next and often most difficult stage is to establish the causes of those gaps, and whether or not the reasons behind them are justified. Many organisations have found this is the stage at which they really do become constrained by the amount of information, particularly historical information, they have available.

Ideally, to understand and establish the justifiability of different levels of reward between individuals doing equal work, information on a wide range of factors such as their starting salaries, previous experience, qualifications, promotion history and performance awards would have to be considered. But to have this quantity of information and to do this level of analysis between all individuals doing equal work, particularly within a large organisation, would be an extremely time-consuming task.

Organisations tend, therefore, to look for general trends and influences that may be behind differences in pay rates and benefits between particular groups at this stage. For example, analyses of starting salaries, rates of progression, performance pay awards, or market pay, by gender, age, ethnicity, disability, etc, would highlight whether any group disproportionately benefited from, or was hindered by, any of these particular aspects or stages in the reward system. If a disproportionate impact was established it would be necessary to consider whether or not there could be an objectively justifiable reason for the variations in pay.

If an organisation is approaching the equal pay review from a narrow legal compliance perspective, and it has found pay gaps and is uncertain of the legal justifiability of them, it may decide to just accept the risk of equal pay claims being brought and to let a tribunal decide. If, however, an organisation has a more holistic approach to the review – while giving some consideration to what the equal pay case law says – it will want to assess whether the factors that have given rise to pay differentials between certain groups are justifiable from the perspective of what its reward strategy says about how reward is going to be determined, and what its diversity strategy says about how it is going to treat people.

For example, when Lloyds TSB found in its equal pay review that the main reason for pay gaps between those doing equal work was length of service, it believed it had to take action, as its declared corporate objective – clearly communicated throughout the organisation – was to create a high-performance culture and to reward employees on the basis of performance and individual contribution, not on service.

Action plans

As the above example illustrates, the extent to which equal pay reviews lead to action depends not only on the potential legal risks the review identifies, but upon the organisation's objectives in undertaking it, and their wider commitment to diversity.

Those that have approached reviews from a legal compliance perspective have tended, if the review has not revealed any clearcut equal pay liabilities, towards not taking any action; by contrast, those that have been motivated to do a review to learn more about the effectiveness and fairness of their reward system have tended to embark upon a range of activities to ensure greater equity in reward.

The actions undertaken do not necessarily involve re-designs of the entire reward system but, at minimum, the review is likely to lead to further questions being asked about how fair the system is and how effectively it is being implemented, and to lead to further investigations and monitoring. As Nic Turner, Shell UK's HR Leader, comments:

The questions you get out of an equal pay review, besides the reassurance there are no gross errors occurring, are what is most useful, because it makes you think more deeply about the whole issue of diversity and reward.

Organisations that have taken action following an equal pay review have often decided to train line managers to improve their skills and knowledge on reward and diversity and have sought to introduce better monitoring of reward decisions. As organisations have introduced greater flexibility into their reward systems in recent years, more responsibility has been devolved to line managers, but many have since found, through doing equal pay reviews, that this is where unjustifiable inequalities arise. As one reward manager commented:

Our pay system is actually pretty sound and doesn't have an inherent gender bias, but we have a pay gap. How does it occur? Every time managers make a discretionary decision.

A diversity manager of another company said one of the major benefits of doing an equal pay review was that:

It sends a message to managers that they need to pay attention to the way in which reward decisions are being made.

In the next chapter we will discuss in more detail some of the actions that can be taken to ensure fairness in reward practice. But whatever reward structures and processes are adopted, it should be remembered that reward systems will never be perfect. Organisations and structures constantly evolve and reward decisions are continually being made that can impact upon internal equity. By examining the distribution of reward at regular intervals, through equal pay reviews, an organisation will be able to take action to correct and improve its reward structure and processes to make them fairer and more effective. As Nic Turner of Shell UK explains:

We've begun, what I would describe, as our perpetual equal pay project.

Equal pay reviews at Nationwide Building Society

Nationwide Building Society has carried out annual equal pay reviews since 2001. Its reviews are very wide-ranging and the analysis includes comparisons of pay and benefits by any combination of gender, full-time or part-time status, length of service, job family, appraisal scores, ad hoc payments, starting salaries, promotion pay and pay for maternity returners, and it is engaged in trying to better understand the effects of ethnicity. It has sought to improve the process each year by seeking to identify individuals with similar characteristics and comparing better matched samples, rather than just comparing averages for broad categories of employees and is currently working with its trade union to enhance the audit.

Paul Bissell, Senior Manager – Rewards, explains:

Equal pay reviews can be self-limiting if people just look at pay as a gender issue, because it isn't.

He adds:

Most organisations have something in their annual report about fairness and valuing people; equal pay reviews are where you put your reputation on the line and prove it.

In its initial reviews, Nationwide found that starting salaries tended to be higher for men; part-timers tended to get lower performance scores than full-timers; and men tended to be more likely to receive ad hoc payments. It has since done work training its recruiters and improving awareness of line managers to ensure they only pay higher starting salaries when objectively justified and that they focus on contribution when assessing performance and are not swayed by stereotypical perceptions of how a job should be done. Starting salaries which are set more than a third of the way between the minimum and the target rate of a pay band now have to be signed off by divisional directors and candidates' previous salaries are checked with their employers.

Endnotes

1   EQUAL PAY TASK FORCE. *Just Pay*. Manchester: EOC, 2001.

2   KINGSMILL, D. *A Review of Women's Employment and Pay*. 2001.

3   SCHÄFER, S., WINTERBOTHAM, M., and McANDREW, F. (IFF), *Equal pay reviews survey 2004*. Manchester: EOC, 2005.

4   CIPD. *Reward management*. CIPD annual survey report, London: CIPD, 2005.

5   ACAS. *Evidence to Women and Work Commission*. London: Acas, 2005.

6   NEATHEY, F., WILLISON, R., AKROYD, K., REGAN, J., and HILL, D., (IES) *Equal pay reviews in practice*. Manchester: EOC, 2005.

7   EOC. *Equal pay, fair pay – A small business guide to effective pay practices*. Manchester: EOC, 2003.

ISBN	Qty	Sales Order
9781843981589	1	F 9754113 1

Customer P/O No		Cust P/O List
524/0028		19.99 GBP

Title: Reward and diversity : making fair pay add up to

Format: P (Paperback)
Author: Brett, Sally.
Publisher: Chartered Institute of Personnel an
Fund:
Location: Library
Loan Type:

Order Specific Instructions

UK 51909001 F

Ship To:
ST HELENS COLLEGE LIBRARY
WATER STREET
ST HELENS
MERSEYSIDE
WA10 1PP

Volume:
Edition:
Year: 2006.
Coutts CN: 5088037

Routing	
Sorting	
Y01H11Z	
Covering — BXAXX	
Despatch	

228169323 ukrwlg48 RC2

- ◘ **Pay and benefits should be determined against relevant job-related criteria and not be influenced by an employee's age, gender, ethnicity, disability, sexual orientation, marital status, religion or belief**

- ◘ **To ensure objectivity in reward system design, job evaluation needs to underpin any grading structure and progression should realistically reflect the time it takes a satisfactory performer to become fully competent and effective in the post**

- ◘ **Line managers need to be trained and given the skills needed to implement reward processes in a fair and non-discriminatory way and their decisions should be monitored**

4 | Fair reward practice

While much attention has been focused on equal pay reviews in recent years and whether or not organisations are carrying them out, equal pay reviews alone do not make an organisation an equal pay or fair pay employer. In this chapter, we look at some of the actions organisations can perform, and have performed, to make reward fairer.

We do not recommend a particular grading structure or set of reward mechanisms that all organisations should adopt, since what is appropriate for one organisation may not be appropriate for another, and developing an effective reward strategy depends very much upon understanding and tailoring the design of the system to the circumstances of the organisation – its business objectives, its culture, the people it is seeking to recruit, and the market it operates in. Instead, we outline some of the issues an organisation needs to consider to make sure its reward system is non-discriminatory and how it can ensure more effective and fairer implementation of reward, whatever its design.

In brief, fair reward practice means having:

- a clear commitment to the principle of fair reward and clarity and transparency about the organisation's general reward principles and aims

- fair and objective processes for determining reward

- monitoring of reward outcomes to ensure the processes are actually operating in a fair and objective way.

> '...equal pay reviews alone do not make an organisation an equal pay or fair pay employer.'

Fair reward principles

Fair reward needs to begin with a commitment to equity in reward, which should incorporate a commitment to the principle of equal pay for equal work. Organisations need then to be clear, and communicate under what circumstances reward will vary for those doing equal work. For example, will reward vary by individual performance or contribution? By competency? Or according to variations in the external market for particular locations or particular jobs? And finally, if variations are to occur, employees need to understand how this fits with the overall business strategy and organisational objectives.

Having this kind of transparency and clarity around the organisation's reward principles and objectives is essential. It shapes individuals' expectations about what to expect from reward and frames the decisions and attitudes of those responsible for implementing it within the organisation.

Fair reward processes

The next element of fair reward practice is to ensure that, as far as is possible, there is objectivity in the methods used for determining reward, so that no individual is treated unfairly because of influences related to their sex, ethnicity, disability, age, religion or belief, sexual orientation, family caring responsibilities or working hours arrangements.

Job evaluation

Job evaluation is the first step in ensuring objectivity. It is essential for establishing where equal work is being performed and should underpin any grading or pay band structure. Job evaluation is therefore the foundation of a fair reward approach.

As already indicated, there are various approaches to job evaluation, and in larger organisations schemes may be very sophisticated and should be analytical and factor-based, as only these would serve as a defence to an equal pay claim. In smaller organisations, however, approaches may need to be simpler, but should still be analytical in nature to reduce the impact of subjective judgements. This could be achieved, for example, by drawing up systematic job descriptions for all the jobs in the organisation – looking at things like responsibilities, tasks, and the level of skill and knowledge needed for each job – and then, by directly comparing the job descriptions, the employer can identify who is doing broadly similar work in terms of the demands made of them and the qualifications and skills needed. (The EOC's equal pay review kit for small employers provides information on establishing equal work in the absence of a job evaluation scheme.[1])

In analytical job evaluation schemes, jobs are broken down into their individual components and are assessed and scored against a range of different factors relating to areas such as responsibility, skill level, and effort. While there are always opportunities for subjectivity to creep into job evaluation, as ultimately the assessments and scoring depend on human judgement, this kind of analytical, factor-by-factor approach is far superior to schemes in which whole jobs are compared and ranked against each other on a 'felt fair' basis. Assessors in analytical factor-based schemes are forced to look at each of the demands of a job in some detail, and are therefore less likely to be swayed by their initial instincts and prejudices, whereas superficial or cosmetic 'felt fair' judgements of whole jobs often end up doing nothing more than reproducing the status quo. Fairness is therefore more likely to be achieved as a result of breaking jobs down into smaller components as it reduces the way in which overall impressions or perceptions – which can be inaccurate – inform the way jobs are valued.

Even where an analytical scheme is used, it is important to give careful consideration to its structure and content to make sure it is relevant, coherent, consistent and fair. If the job evaluation scheme itself is inherently biased, it will not ensure fairness. Ideally, the same job evaluation scheme should apply to all employees, so all instances of equal work across the organisation are established. Careful consideration also needs to be given to the factors against which jobs are going to be assessed, particularly if there are a wide variety of jobs, so that factors that are relevant to all jobs are included. For example, EOC guidance[2] shows how in some job evaluation schemes, factors like 'physical effort' are included or given greater weight, while 'emotional effort' is overlooked or given minimal weighting. Where this happens, emotionally demanding, often female-dominated, jobs receive lower rankings than physically demanding, often male-dominated, jobs.

In terms of administering a job evaluation scheme, evaluations should be carried out by more than one person to gain more objectivity, and those responsible for evaluations should be trained in equality issues and should be aware of how bias can arise, and their own tendencies for stereotyping and subjectivity. It is also advisable to have evaluation panels and appeals committees, which are representative of the different parts of the workforce and the diversity of employees in the organisation. Finally, how the scheme is operating in practice should be regularly reviewed, and re-evaluations and appeals should be monitored to make sure the system works effectively. Most jobs are by their nature subject to change, development and growth and such changes need to be captured by reviewing job descriptions regularly and ensuring jobs are properly evaluated and graded.

> *'Ideally, the same job evaluation scheme should apply to all employees, so all instances of equal work across the organisation are established.'*

Grading structures

When translating job evaluation scores into a grading structure, bias can be introduced if care is not exercised over where the boundary lines between grades are drawn. It is often hard to distinguish natural breaks in the distribution of job evaluation scores and any decision that results in a job dominated by mainly female staff or ethnic minority staff falling one side of the line, and a job dominated mainly by men or white staff falling on the other side, needs to be questioned and investigated further to make sure decisions have not been influenced by stereotypical thinking or prejudice.

A grading structure with a small number of broad pay bands may make decisions of where lines are drawn easier as there may be more obvious natural breaks in the point scores. Broad bands also have the advantage that grade boundaries do not have to be as frequently reassessed when jobs change and are re-evaluated, compared to when there is a narrow graded structure.

The disadvantage with broad bands from an equity perspective though, is that because many jobs of quite different sizes can fall within the same salary range, it can be harder to ensure equal pay for equal work, and to understand the rationale behind any of the variations that arise within bands, compared to narrow graded structures, where there is a much more direct and transparent translation of job evaluation scores into salaries.

Progression

How individuals progress within grades and pay bands is something that some organisations have revised in light of findings from equal pay reviews and concerns about equity. In general, with the recent focus on equal pay, progression has become more structured and transparent, and stronger guidance has been given to line managers on how fast employees should be progressed to what is considered a fully effective rate for the job, providing their performance is satisfactory.

Broad bands

Organisations with broad pay bands have sometimes found that progression has been too slow for new entrants. They have been unable to catch up with their longer serving colleagues or with those who were recruited or promoted into the pay bands on higher salaries, even when they have shown an equivalent level of performance and competence in post.

This kind of persistent inequality typically occurs when progression rises are expressed as a percentage of existing salary and the same percentage goes to everyone who has achieved the same level of performance, regardless of their position in a pay band. Flat-rate awards for different levels of performance, or performance pay matrices that provide higher rises to those lower down the pay band for the same level of performance, will provide faster catch-up and should narrow differentials between individuals at a rate that more realistically reflects the time taken to develop competence in a particular role.

In addition, some organisations in recent years have introduced ceilings on progression, so that progression occurs at a rate depending on the individual's performance until they reach a target salary level which is deemed the fully effective or market rate for a particular job. After that point, if an individual shows good performance or contribution in a particular year, they receive an unconsolidated bonus payment as a reward, rather than higher basic pay. This brake on progression recognises that, if performance continues to be rewarded with consolidated payments, pay gaps between those with shorter and longer service will persist, despite the fact that the gap between their level of contribution has closed.

Tackling equal pay at Lloyds TSB

When Lloyds TSB carried out an equal pay review it found that the key structural factor that lay behind pay gaps between individuals doing equal work was length of service. This concerned the reward and diversity teams because the intention of the pay system had been to reward everyone equitably on the basis of their performance and contribution, and not simply on long service.

Jonathan Lazenby, HR business partner for diversity and equality, explains:

The intention of our pay system was that we were paying for performance, but what happened – and I think this could be a problem for any organisation with long-serving staff – is, when staff are near what is deemed to be the going rate for the job, very few managers feel comfortable saying "you are a valued member of staff, you do a great job, but you are being paid at the going rate, so I'm not going to pay you any more this year". It's a difficult message to give and receive. Generally, most people tended to get an annual pay award. Then year on year their pay crept up and eventually they were being paid noticeably above the going rate (and other colleagues with shorter service), even though their performance in terms of contribution might not merit that level of pay.

Lloyds TSB, in light of the findings of its equal pay review, decided it had to strengthen the link between performance and reward. 'Our defining principle behind all this was to create an inclusive meritocracy', says Jonathan Lazenby. To achieve this end:

◘ the pay structure was made more transparent

◘ line managers were given training on equal pay and rewarding performance

◘ information on the new pay structure and reward principles was distributed among employees

◘ annual organisation-wide equal pay reviews were introduced.

The pay structure had previously comprised a series of broad pay bands with salary minimums and no maximums. Following the equal pay review, to create more openness and transparency in reward, each pay band was divided into three zones – the primary, market and high-performance zones – and the salaries for the top and bottom of each zone were published. This gives employees a clear indication of what the normal rate of pay is for someone who is developing in a role, someone who is fully effective in a role, and someone who is consistently displaying superior performance in a role. The new structure also gives line managers more of a guide in terms of the priorities for progression and how to manage pay expectations.

About 1,000 of the first-line recommending managers were sent on a one-day training course prior to the new pay structure being introduced. The training covered the basics of equal pay, law and compliance issues, and how the previous pay system had given rise to what were considered unjustifiable inequalities based on length of service. This was then linked to the reasons for introducing the new pay structure and Lloyds TSB's drive to become a high-performance organisation, in which people's salaries were linked to ongoing performance and contribution, not length of service. Managers were then given a number of case studies to examine and were asked what the pay rise ought to be and how they would communicate that to the employee.

Polly Shepherd, reward manager, sums up Lloyds TSB's progress:

We have a transparent structure now and there is clearer dialogue between line managers and staff… We're acting on principles we believe in. We're not just doing it, but we're communicating with staff about equal pay. And, although we're giving some hard messages about performance, we're giving very positive messages too. The feedback that we're getting is that this clear approach is much better.

Source: *IDS Diversity at Work No.14*

Service-related progression

As can be gathered from the above discussion, the justifiability of rewarding length of service has been brought into question by the recent focus on equal pay (and in the development of age legislation). This is because the additional service that is being rewarded does not always translate into greater effectiveness or competence in the role. For example, there would be few jobs in which paying someone with 15 years' service more than someone with 12 years' service could be justified, in terms of it automatically leading to greater effectiveness or better performance.

Furthermore, service-related progression has a potentially discriminatory impact on both women and younger workers as they are less likely to be able to achieve long service because of career breaks or a shorter employment history. Organisations, therefore need, to be careful about using long incremental or service-related pay scales.

Many civil service organisations have recently abandoned the link with seniority and have introduced shorter progression scales, in which there are typically about five to eight steps through which staff progress annually, provided their performance is shown to be satisfactory. The Cabinet Office report[3] summarising the results of equal pay reviews that were carried out across the civil service in 2003 said that:

The shortening of pay ranges and the move to clear and transparent pay progression systems was identified as the most effective action to reduce the gender pay gap by virtually all departments and agencies.

The draft regulations outlawing age discrimination due to come into effect from October 2006 mean that in the future there will have to be objective justification of any link between length of service and reward beyond five years. The consultation on the age Regulations states that:

During the first few years of service using length of service as a criterion for awarding or increasing benefits is justified – we consider five years a reasonable limit. The age Regulations will provide a complete exemption for this period.

If an employer wishes to continue progressing individuals according to length of service after five years' service, then they will have to provide an objective justification for doing so, which means they will have to show that such a method of reward supports the achievement of a legitimate business aim and that there is no less discriminatory way of them achieving that aim.

What the draft age Regulations say about pay and benefits

Service-related pay and benefits

Requiring employees to have a certain length of service before pay or benefits are given or increased will often amount to indirect age discrimination, as some age groups are likely to have longer service than others. Maintaining service-related pay and benefits will be unlawful when age discrimination legislation takes effect from 1 October 2006, unless they can be objectively justified (ie they are a proportionate means of achieving a legitimate business aim).

However, it is proposed that there will be two specific exemptions to the requirement for objective justification. These are:

◘ any length-of-service requirement of five years or less will be allowed to continue

◘ any length-of-service requirement that mirrors a similar requirement in a statutory benefit (eg

redundancy payments or the National Minimum Wage) will be allowed to continue.

Pensions

The age Regulations will effectively exempt certain age-related rules or practices in occupational pension schemes. These include:

◘ closing pension schemes or parts of pension schemes to new members

◘ the use of minimum and maximum ages for admission to pension schemes

◘ setting different ages of admission to a pension scheme for different groups of employees

◘ both age-related and flat-rate employer contributions into pension schemes

◘ setting the level of pension benefits by reference to years of service.

Starting salaries

After differences in rates of progression, the second most common source of unjustifiable pay gaps found by employers that have done equal pay reviews are differences in starting salaries. In many instances, there is a degree of flexibility and negotiation around starting salaries and individuals often expect this. Negotiation may be necessary for the organisation to get their chosen candidate, and pragmatic concerns over filling a vacancy with the best candidate within a certain time frame often override concerns about internal pay relativities. Negotiations can also be made more difficult if a candidate's previous employer had a strategy of paying above market rates.

Many organisations have found that women tend to fare worse than men in such negotiation processes and it is possible that other groups, such as black and minority ethnic employees, disabled employees and older workers, may similarly suffer a detriment, as they may not feel in a strong enough position to ask for a higher salary.

> *'To avoid the risk of discrimination, line managers and recruiters must be made aware of the requirements of equal pay and anti-discrimination legislation.'*

In the case of women, the reasons for them achieving lower starting salaries have been variously put down to: men being better negotiators than women; men being more money-oriented while women look to other elements of the package such as work–life balance; women being unfairly penalised as they are more likely to be earning less than men in their existing job or, if they are returning to the labour market after a break, their last salary will be behind that of other candidates. Employers should, therefore, be cautious about using a person's pay history to determine their value to the organisation and be more transparent about the rate on offer for the job they want to fill.

To avoid the risk of discrimination, line managers and recruiters must be made aware of the requirements of equal pay and anti-discrimination legislation. They need to be reminded of the criteria and circumstances under which the organisation is willing to offer higher starting salaries, and to be conscious of their own potential to stereotype. For example, many line managers may expect men to ask for more and may enter negotiations being prepared to move their initial offer upwards, but when they are negotiating with female candidates they may emphasise other benefits, like family-friendly policies, and react negatively if a woman asks for more money. Starting salaries, if set by line managers, also need to be reviewed centrally.

If progression is not structured towards an eventual harmonisation for all entrants to an effective rate for the job, mechanisms need to be built into the reward system to allow for regular reviews and reassessments of an individual's current value to the organisation, as otherwise gaps in starting salaries will persist for many years into the future. It should be remembered that those who have been internally promoted to higher level positions often miss out on the external market premium paid to attract outsiders, and unless there are regular reviews of salary levels and internal relativities, they will never make up that differential, even if their contribution proves to be more valuable.

Finally, there are circumstances when organisations may have to allow more leeway for negotiation and take more of a risk to recruit an individual they believe is the most talented for a particular role. This is likely to be the case when making high-level appointments or appointing to specialist positions where the market value of certain individuals is very high. In these instances, to further diversity and to minimise organisation-wide pay gaps arising, employers should make every effort to consider a diverse range of candidates for the job. They should also consider offering more innovative reward packages, including work–life balance options, rather than just focusing on, and negotiating over, the money on offer.

Market pay

Market forces and the need to pay more to recruit and retain those in occupations or locations where there are skill or labour shortages is one of the most common reasons why organisations feel they need to deviate from the principle of equal pay for work of equal value. And the market forces argument has sometimes been accepted as a genuine and material factor defence to an equal pay claim – though sometimes it has not.

The difficulty in justifying market rates from a fair reward perspective is that the market is not perfect and does not treat all individuals in an objective and fair way. What constitutes the market or 'going rate' for a particular job is not just the supply and demand for a particular set of skills. Various research has shown market rates to be biased; for example, jobs dominated by women tend to be paid less than jobs dominated by men

despite demanding similar levels of skill, effort and responsibility, and despite experiencing similar recruitment and retention pressures. This is because:

- there has been a traditional undervaluing of 'women's work' in society

- there used to be a belief that 'a man's wage is a family wage' and this has left a legacy which has boosted the pay of traditionally male-dominated jobs

- and there has often been greater collective bargaining strength in a number of key male-dominated sectors.

'The difficulty in justifying market rates from a fair reward perspective is that the market is not perfect and does not treat [everyone] in an objective and fair way.'

So bearing in mind that market rates are not always an objective reflection of relative recruitment and retention pressures but that there are a number of other more subjective factors that feed into the determination of market rates, which can have discriminatory consequences for different segments of the workforce, organisations need to take care when slavishly following what others pay in setting their own rates. In some instances, the organisation may feel that paying lower rates to a job which is of equal value to others in the organisation, particularly if it is dominated by women or minority ethnic workers, just because others in the external market do, is not appropriate as it goes against its corporate values. For example, Oxfam was uncomfortable paying its charity shop managers, who were mainly female, at the market rate, as the market rate for such jobs was lower than those jobs of a similar level of responsibility within Oxfam. It said:

In this case, market forces are not considered a valid reason for pay differences, as they may be based on preconceptions about the value of "women's work", which constitutes discrimination.[4]

Although a single organisation cannot always buck what is happening in the external market, patterns of discrimination are likely to be reinforced if the organisation relies solely on line managers' or employees' perceptions of what is happening in the market and how much a job should be paid. For example, around the time of the millennium, there was a high demand for IT skills and a great deal of publicity about how IT staff were in short supply. Salaries rose at that time as a result and it is likely that most people still think IT staff should be paid more relative to other occupations requiring similar levels of skill, responsibility and effort, even though the market for their skills has considerably altered.

In recent years, many organisations have taken a more rigorous approach to establishing what the market rate is for a particular job, and are more regularly reviewing and adjusting their pay rates in line with movements in the market. Most do this by subscribing to a number of salary surveys and regularly benchmarking their rates against others. If such an approach is taken, organisations need to ensure that the process is transparent and that similar treatment is accorded to all. The comparisons that are made with the external market must be relevant – ie they should cover the appropriate local and/or functional labour markets from which the organisation would seek to recruit (and from a diversity perspective, the organisation should also question the validity of its existing recruitment pools and whether or not they should be widened). CIPD evidence in the survey published in 2005, *Recruitment, retention and turnover*,[5] showed more organisations were developing diverse approaches to recruitment to be successful and attracting and retaining talent.

It is also important for organisations to remember why they opted to pay at market rates in the first place. Normally, it is to ensure that they can continue to recruit and retain staff. In which case, there is other human capital data, beyond pay benchmark information, that is relevant to determining relative recruitment and retention pressures, such as the number of applicants per job, reasons for job offers being turned down, and the reasons given for leaving jobs or considering leaving the organisation in exit interviews or staff surveys. Considering a broader range of indicators will give a more reliable and objective assessment of what is happening in the external market, and the justifiability of any internal pay variations.

Recruitment and retention supplements in the NHS

Under the new *Agenda for Change* pay system designed to ensure equal pay for equal work in the NHS, local employers can increase pay for certain jobs by paying recruitment and retention premiums if they feel the market calls for it. However, to ensure consistency and objectivity, the following steps should be taken before making such pay additions:

◘ to assess the nature and extent of recruitment and retention pressures, the number of applicants, relevant national vacancy data, and local labour market information need to be considered

◘ non-pay improvements to the employment package (eg childcare or training opportunities) should be offered first, if it is believed these could improve recruitment and retention

◘ jobs should be re-advertised in alternative media if it is believed this could result in more suitable applicants, or at a later date, if there is to be an expected increase in supply (eg new trainees).

In addition, once recruitment and retention premiums have been made they should be reviewed annually and, where it is believed that labour market circumstances have changed and that they are no longer necessary in order to recruit and retain, they should be phased out.

Performance pay

Variations in pay according to performance will only be fair if performance is assessed against objective and transparent criteria, and if those making the assessments and the pay decisions do so in an unbiased way.

When designing any performance management system, those responsible for diversity and equal opportunities should be consulted and involved in the process to alert the organisation to any potentially discriminatory criteria. Ensuring output-based performance criteria are SMART (specific, measurable, achievable, relevant and timed) will improve objectivity. In addition, employees should participate in the setting of their own objectives, rather than just having them handed down to them, to ensure they are realistic and achievable and perceived as being fair.

If employees are assessed against behaviour-based performance criteria, then the organisation needs to integrate its approach to diversity in shaping these criteria. For example, it needs to be very clear in setting out the kinds of behaviour the organisation aspires to encourage and that which it will not tolerate, to ensure behaviour fits with its core diversity values, such as respect for difference and equity. But, organisations must also be careful not to be over-prescriptive in describing different kinds of positive behaviour, as valuing diversity means accepting that there are usually many different and equally acceptable ways of achieving the same goal.

Most performance management tends to fall down on the implementation rather than the design stage. Despite setting objectives, non-discriminatory criteria and having structured frameworks for appraisals, the final assessment and judgement on the appraisal rating, and the level of pay award, is informed by individuals so subjectivity and bias can creep in. Line managers need to be trained to understand bias and how to avoid it and how to performance manage a diverse workforce in ways that increase awareness about preconceptions of how a job should be done. This kind of training should be regular, not just a one-off event. It needs to be repeated regularly to refresh line managers' knowledge and awareness and to provide new line managers with the same level of understanding.

Finally, before appraisal scores are translated into performance awards, the decisions should be centrally reviewed either by HR, managers' peer groups, or by more senior managers, to check for any indications of unfair bias by sex, ethnicity, disability, age, and to ensure there is consistency and fairness in the way appraisals are being carried out, and the ratings and awards that are being made.

Benefits

As well as ensuring fairness in the distribution of pay, organisations need to assess the justifiability of the allocation of benefits, again, not just from a legal perspective, but from a diversity perspective, too. For example, while some employers may have to adjust their pension schemes to provide survivor benefits to same-sex partners who are in a civil partnership, is it really acceptable for non-married partners, whatever their sexual orientation, to be excluded from benefits that are provided to married partners in an organisation that says it recognises diversity? And have organisations considered offering Muslim employees the opportunity to invest in Sharia-compliant pension funds, to which a number of pension providers are now offering access, through occupational pension schemes?

Sexual orientation and benefits provision

The restriction of benefits to married couples is one of the most obvious examples of indirect sexual orientation discrimination. However, the Employment Equality (Sexual Orientation) Regulations 2003 expressly provide that such discrimination is lawful. Regulation 25 states that:

Nothing shall render unlawful anything which prevents or restricts access to a benefit by reference to marital status.

In 2004, a group of unions unsuccessfully challenged the Regulation 25 exception in the High Court. They subsequently lodged an appeal, but withdrew it in light of the Civil Partnership Act. Under the Act, which came into force in December 2005, same-sex couples who form a civil partnership will have parity of treatment in a wide range of legal matters with those opposite-sex couples who enter into a civil marriage. To reflect this, the Government amended the Sexual Orientation Regulations to require that civil partners and spouses should be treated in the same way in relation to workplace benefits.

Pensions

Pensions are an element of reward to which there is unequal access and levels of provision in many organisations, as the more generous final salary pension schemes have been closed to new entrants or have been altered to offer them reduced benefits. Given the financial difficulties that many occupational pension schemes are facing, some of these actions have been necessary to protect the savings of existing scheme members, and certain service and age-related rules and practices in occupational pension schemes have been exempted from the draft Regulations on age discrimination. However, organisations need to ensure, when making decisions on the future of pensions, that they are providing a solution or range of solutions that treat all existing and future employees as fairly as possible in the prevailing circumstances, and that wide disparities in treatment and the value of benefits being offered should be avoided as far as possible.

Equity in other HR processes

As outlined above, there are many ways in which bias can emerge in reward structures and processes themselves, and there is much that can be done to make them fairer. But inequalities in reward can also arise because of unfairness and bias in other people-management and development processes and decision-making which inform reward systems and processes. For example, if there is no equity in how individuals are treated in other areas, such as promotion and selection, training and development, flexible working, and rostering, there will be unequal access to the opportunities that lead to increased reward. As Denise Kingsmill said:

Comparisons of pay provide an initial indicator which opens the door onto a whole range of employment and human capital issues.

If inequities in other people-management and development processes are uncovered through an equal pay review, these need to be addressed by diversity and HR specialists. Progress in tackling disparities will be highlighted by the way the pay gaps narrow over subsequent years. For example, one retailer found, through its equal pay review, that those at head office were not progressing as quickly as those in its retail network, as they were not always receiving the same training and development opportunities. It has, therefore, subsequently planned action to provide these employees with similar training and development opportunities as those in the retail network.

Fair reward outcomes

Achieving fair reward is not a finite project with one beginning and one ending – it is an ongoing process. Once the policies have been adopted and the reward structure and processes designed and implemented to ensure greater fairness, the outcomes need to be regularly monitored to check that they are fair and that the processes are operating in the way they were intended. Equal pay reviews should be carried out at regular intervals, but organisations also need to put in place mechanisms to monitor the outcomes of different reward processes on an ongoing basis. For example, organisations should consider monitoring the following by sex, ethnicity, disability, age and so on:

◻ starting salaries

◻ promotion salaries

◻ performance pay awards

◻ bonus payments

◻ access to overtime and unsociable hours payments

◻ recruitment and retention or market supplements.

Regular monitoring of reward decisions to check for any bias enables an organisation to correct and adjust any potentially discriminatory or unfair

decisions before they are translated into changes in reward. The information gathered from an ongoing monitoring of reward decisions will improve and speed up the equal pay review process, as it will be easier for organisations to trace back why different reward decisions were made, how they have led to differences in reward levels, and whether or not they are justifiable and continue to be so.

Endnotes

1 EOC. *Equal pay, fair pay – A small business guide to effective pay practices.* Manchester: EOC, 2003.

2 EOC. *Good Practice Guide: Job evaluation schemes free of sex bias.* Available from www.eoc.org.uk

3 *Civil service equal pay action plans summary.* London: Cabinet Office, 2003.

4 Oxfam's *Links* journal. April 2004 issue.

5 *Recruitment, retention and turnover.* CIPD annual survey report. London: CIPD, 2005.

- ◘ To realise the full benefits of a fair reward approach on employee engagement and motivation, organisations must provide clear and effective communications about it.

- ◘ It is clear that while organisations may be carrying out equal pay reviews to improve their employer image they are often failing to communicate this – sometimes through fear of exposing sensitive information or raising expectations.

- ◘ Listening to employees and seeking their opinions on reward can provide valuable information on how the reward strategy is working in practice and alert the organisation to any unfairness or failures in communication.

5 | Reward communications

Effective communication on reward is essential if an organisation is to realise the full benefits of fair reward on employee engagement and motivation. However, many organisations are uncomfortable about openly communicating on reward issues and some even positively encourage a culture of secrecy around it. Below, we look at what needs to be communicated and how, for employees to understand the organisation's commitment to fair reward and the measures taken to achieve it. Clearly, where the employment relationship is adversarial, steps towards being more open about reward should be taken gradually, and the organisation should focus on fostering a more positive employee relations climate in the first instance.

Corporate communications

What needs to be communicated at a corporate level is the organisation's commitment to fairness in reward, including its commitment to equal pay for equal work, and the criteria against which it may vary reward and how this variation supports the achievement of its corporate objectives. Employees should additionally be given information on the general structure of reward – the grades or pay bands and associated salaries – and the criteria and mechanisms for progression through that structure. There should be similar, easily accessible information on how the other elements of pay, such as bonus schemes and market supplements, operate. This information should be written in jargon-free language that will make sense to, and engage, employees – it should not be regurgitated from information written for reward and HR professionals.

Corporate level communications need not go into great detail about how the various reward processes work, but there does need to be transparency about the essential principles, characteristics and aims that shape them. For example, employees who are told that pay is set against market rates may want to know that the organisation regularly benchmarks all its pay rates and looks at relevant labour market and vacancy data, to make sure the organisation's policy on market pay is credible. Similarly, if people are told that their annual pay rises reflect their performance in a particular year, they are not likely to feel awards are fair unless they understand how their performance was assessed and how it was translated into a performance award.

In a research project funded by the Economic and Social Research Council on employee perceptions of fair pay, Dr. Annette Cox from Manchester

Business School found that perceptions of fairness depended less on the particular reward structure or mechanisms that an organisation has adopted, and more on how well they were communicated. For example, she found that in one financial organisation with a complex bonus scheme, the scheme was perceived as *fair* because, thanks to good communication, employees had a good understanding of how it operated. But in another organisation, straightforward cost-of-living pay rises were perceived as *unfair* as they had not been properly communicated by the organisation or trade union.

> '*...when implementing job evaluation to ensure equal pay for work of equal value, some employees will inevitably see their jobs downgraded and themselves becoming worse off...*'

Communicating on fair reward

As well as transparency around general reward objectives and processes, organisations should be prepared to explain and show that the reward structure, processes, and actions they have adopted are fair, and they should be prepared to deal with competing notions of fairness. This is particularly important if the organisation is making changes to the current reward system, as employees are likely to be suspicious and to perceive any change to their existing pay and benefits as unfair, even if they are being carried out to provide greater objectivity and equity in reward. Some will wonder what the catch is unless communications are good.

For example, when implementing job evaluation to ensure equal pay for work of equal value, some employees will inevitably see their jobs downgraded and themselves becoming worse off and so they, and the rest of the workforce, need to understand how the new structure provides a fairer and more objective basis for determining reward. In such circumstances, it is usually appropriate to offer some sort of pay protection for a limited period of time to the affected individuals, as immediate pay cuts will almost always be perceived as being unfair, and undermine what the organisation is trying to achieve, in terms of employee engagement, when moving to a new system.

Equal pay reviews

Organisations are missing an opportunity to engage employees and increase trust and perceptions of fairness, by not being open and honest in communicating the initiatives they are undertaking to ensure equal pay and fair reward or involving employees in their design. Ironically, many employers have undertaken equal pay reviews because they are seen as being good practice and they want to improve their image and employment brand but they have not informed their employees that they have done one. As an HR manager of a voluntary sector organisation said:

From a presentational point of view doing an equal pay review demonstrates best practice – it shows that we are mindful of these things and we do attach importance to equity and fairness and how we reward people. It has been very useful from that point of view. Although if you ask people in this organisation 'are you aware that an equal pay review has been done?' I doubt many people would have a clue either way. We didn't communicate that we'd done it and I don't know why that was the case.

One of the reasons why some organisations have shied away from openly informing employees that a review has been carried out, is their concern about reactions to negative findings. As one reward manager commented:

How do you say 'we've only got a pay gap of 5 per cent in favour of men'? This will alienate the majority of our workforce who are female, which is not what we want to do.

However, at BT, information summarising the findings of their reviews and the actions taken to ensure equal pay has been made available to employees and the public. Caroline Waters, Director of People Networks at BT, believes that informing employees that an equal pay review has been carried out has a positive impact, as it clearly shows the organisation's commitment to equity. She believes that this is the case, even when a review finds pay gaps, as BT's did, so long as the organisation clearly communicates not just the findings of the review, but the actions that are being taken to correct any gaps.

This kind of openness could be particularly important if the organisation wants to maintain employee engagement and commitment following corrective action. Increasing an individual's pay because of equal pay concerns, without adequately and carefully explaining why such action is being taken, may result in the affected employee dwelling on the unfairness of the previous situation, rather than appreciating the organisation's commitment to fairness and its willingness to be honest and address the problem.

However, in some instances, where there has been an adversarial employee relations environment and equal pay reviews reveal possible inequitable treatment, organisations may want time to formulate an action plan and to address the problem areas before it makes an open commitment to fair reward. If they believe that such a commitment will be viewed with suspicion or hostility, then the organisation needs to consider broader issues of how to create a more positive employee relations environment, where there is trust and credibility, before launching into communications on fair reward in order to ensure that, when it does communicate on fair reward, there is substantive action and evidence to support its words.

Individual communications

As well as corporate level communications on overall reward principles, structures and processes, individual employees need to understand what their particular salary level, pay rise, and benefits package is, and how it was determined within the wider system. Perceptions of unfairness can arise about an individual's level of reward because of a lack of knowledge or understanding about the overall value and design of the package they are receiving.

Rather than just provide salary slips and brief letters informing employees that their salary has increased by x per cent from a certain date or that they have received £x as a bonus award, providing supplementary information on the overall grading structure, the matrix for determining pay rises that year, or the targets and associated levels of payment within bonus schemes, will remind employees of how and why the reward system operates, and will help them understand the connection between their efforts and the reward they are receiving. Regular total reward statements, which itemise all the pay and benefits an employee receives, and the value of them, can also ensure a much better understanding of the whole package.

Finally, an important but often overlooked element in securing employee engagement and commitment through reward is communicating to employees when they have performed well, what was good about their performance and indicating why they are being rewarded.

Line managers

Some of the most important communications shaping employees' expectations of reward is with their line managers. Line managers are often uncomfortable openly discussing reward with their subordinates for fear that it might de-motivate them, and they may suggest to staff that more reward is available in order to recruit and retain or motivate them. Line managers may even blame HR for why they are not in a position to offer more money, even if it is not warranted by an individual's contribution, rather than have an honest discussion about pay. While line managers may fear the short-term impact on employees' motivation, they need to understand too that if they create unrealistic expectations, which are not then fulfilled, trust in the organisation and employees' sense of fairness will be severely undermined over the longer term.

Line managers should, therefore, be regularly updated on the reward strategy and how reward processes work. They also need to be given adequate training and support to ensure they have the skills and confidence needed to have open, and sometimes difficult, discussions about reward with their staff. When Lloyds TSB revised its performance-based reward system in light of the findings of its equal pay review, it recognised that getting line managers to hold challenging discussions with individuals about their performance and reward was one of the hardest, but most important elements of the changes they made.

Listening to employees

Communication is a two-way process that involves listening as well as talking. This means that organisations need to be willing to listen to employees' opinions about fair reward and take these into account. Doing equal pay reviews, identifying inequalities, and taking action to make reward processes more objective and fair, is one side of the equation; the other is using employees views and ideas to shape their design, and checking that employees understand why actions have been taken and that they are perceived as fair. Only then will reward and diversity practice make progress towards the shared aim of engaging and motivating employees.

Organisations should consider including questions such as 'do you think you are fairly rewarded for the job that you do?' in employee attitude surveys. Responses will alert organisations to any major problems with reward or reward communications. Information from such regular surveys will provide a yardstick for progress on fair reward, alongside the findings from equal pay reviews on pay gap changes.

Focus groups and intranet forums on reward can also provide valuable information about the ways in which reward affects different groups of employees. Employees themselves are often well aware of where the inequities in reward lie before the organisation seeks to tackle the issue. Do not underestimate the extent to which employees talk about pay, despite the apparent secrecy and non-disclosure that exists at a corporate level. For example, a manager from a small manufacturing company in Wales found when he presented the results of the equal pay review and the proposals for a new fairer grading structure to employees, that employees had long been aware of the inequities that had existed in the previous system. He explained:

We thought it was extremely important to present our findings to all employees, to explain precisely how we classified each role and the criteria used and what we hoped to achieve in terms of fairness in pay. The feedback I got amazed me, each person seemed to know exactly what their colleagues took home every week and even though the differences were slight, the depth of feeling for those earning slightly less went far beyond the monetary values involved. For them it was a question of their worth to the company, they felt less respected and undervalued in the role they performed and as a result were de-motivated.

> **'Communication is a two-way process that involves listening as well as talking.'**

Hopefully, the overall willingness of organisations to communicate and listen to staff on issues such as equal pay and fairness in reward should increase as organisations grow more confident, through doing equal pay reviews, implementing fair reward practices, and monitoring reward outcomes, that how they are rewarding people in practice is fair, and that it does indeed support business objectives.

BT communicates on fair reward

Caroline Waters, BT's Director of People Networks, believes that communicating with employees on fair reward is vital. She explains:

We don't believe that people are going to come and work for you if they don't believe they are going to be fairly treated. Being able to talk to people very openly about reward is all part of that.

We've just rolled out something called the New Reward Framework at BT. We're just at the stage of explaining to everyone what it means and we are using every piece of technology available to do that. All of the information is on the intranet; we hold monthly web chats; we have focus groups; we have local communication plans and national communication plans. We canvass people about the language they use to talk about these issues – there's an HR language that talks about reward, but employees still say 'pay, tell me about my pay', so you can find information on the website under the words employees would use as well.

Everything's simple and engaging. All line managers are also thoroughly briefed so that they can confidently answer questions on reward.

The core principle in everything that we do is equity. We mention it in everything that we do. We have a document called The way we work *and it's absolutely at the heart of that. So fairness and meritocracy are the principles that are most often quoted.*

If you're worried about communicating on equal pay and fair reward, my advice is to first, listen to your employees and what they have to say.

BT also communicates its approach to equal pay and fair reward to the wider world and the following information appears on its corporate website:

Our approach to equal pay encompasses gender, ethnic origin and disability. We have played an active and constructive role in the gender pay debate over a number of years. Our previous reports show how BT's position has evolved. Equal pay is an increasingly sophisticated issue in the UK. In the 2005 financial year, BT contributed to the Confederation of British Industry (CBI) submission to the Women and Work Commission.

Detailed pay-gap audits undertaken in recent years have revealed a persisting gap in pay between men and women. We believe that one reason is the legacy from the days when our workforce was split between engineers (primarily male) and clerks and operators (mainly female). Pay levels for the two groups were largely developed separately. Other reasons in the UK outlined in the CBI submission, include:

- *career choices and early stereotyping*
- *gender bias in vocational choice*
- *educational achievements of older women*
- *caring responsibilities*
- *lack of family friendly policies*
- *early specialisation.*

BT continues to address these issues holistically. We have Board support to close the pay gap and our pay review processes include guidance on creating a fair and equitable reward system based on performance. All team members (non-managerial grades) are now on the same pay structure and this has significantly reduced the scope for inequality.

Equal pay activities

In the 2005 financial year, we introduced a new reward framework of 300 market-based roles in 18 different families covering about 37,500 employees worldwide. Pay, bonuses and benefits are comparable with the market rate. The introduction of market packages around the world will be phased in during the 2006 financial year. In June 2004, we introduced bonus scorecards for about 20,000 UK employees for calculating bonus payments.

The framework will allow more consistent reward decisions to be made, based on an individual's value in the job market, combined with their contribution to BT's success. It will also form a key component of our analysis of equal pay issues for this group of employees. In addition, over recent years we have:

- *changed our promotion remuneration procedures, particularly in management grades, from a percentage of base salary to a comparison with peers and the market*

- *focused our pay review on the lower end of our pay scales, where there are likely to be more women*

- *carried out a pay audit following each pay review, based on key measures agreed with our unions, maintaining a dialogue on all equality matters. The 2004 BT budget in the UK for equal pay was £3.4 million*

- *recognised work–life balance as a key enabler to eliminating some of the barriers that may be slowing the progress of women in the workforce.*

- ◘ **Pay and benefits can be designed to attract a more diverse workforce.**

- ◘ **Adopting diversity-related targets or competencies with a link to pay can help establish a culture in which diversity is valued.**

- ◘ **An organisation that recognises individual diversity should consider adopting flexible benefits and a total reward approach**

6 | Diversity through reward

As well as ensuring that the design and operation of the reward system is non-discriminatory and treats all individuals fairly, organisations need to consider how their reward system supports their wider commitment to diversity and its objectives of recognising difference and creating an inclusive working environment.

Attracting diversity

Organisations with workforces that are unrepresentative of the diversity that exists in the wider population might want to re-assess the reward they are offering to see what can be done to appeal to, and to better meet the needs of, those that are currently under-represented. For example, if an organisation is very male-dominated, it may decide more could be done to improve its family-friendly benefits or flexible working opportunities in order to boost its image among women. Ford Motor Company[1], as part of a series of measures to attract more women into the automotive engineering sector, greatly enhanced its maternity benefits to include 52 weeks' maternity leave on full pay, making it one of the most generous packages in the country and attracting good publicity around it.

The ageing population and the need to attract or maintain older workers in employment, has similarly led to some organisations tailoring benefits to their specific needs and lifestyle choices. For example, Asda launched a 'Goldies' initiative to encourage more over-50s back into work and, as part of that, introduced 'grandparent's leave', providing one week's unpaid leave to support the arrival of a new grandchild, and 'Benidorm leave', which allows employees over 50 to take unpaid leave of up to three months.

Promoting diversity

As well as using reward to appeal to different under-represented groups and to create greater diversity in the workforce, reward can also be used to facilitate culture change. If an organisation has adopted a performance-related pay system in the belief that it will motivate employees to behave in a certain way and to work towards specific goals, and they have professed a commitment to creating an inclusive and diverse workplace, then consideration needs to be given to the kind of actions and behaviours that are being rewarded, and to whether or not reward should be given for diversity-related achievements as well.

One HR manager from a pharmaceutical company cited the very results-driven, performance-related pay system it previously had as a barrier to implementing diversity, as it encouraged senior staff and managers to behave in a macho, individualistic manner, concerned only with what they were achieving rather than how they were achieving it, and how they were treating their assistants and subordinates in the process. It subsequently introduced more behaviour-related rewards through a competency-based scheme, which helped create a more positive environment for the implementation of its diversity strategy.

'If they [diversity measures] are not realistic and achievable, there could be a backlash against the whole diversity programme.'

At London Underground[2], a specific diversity competence was introduced as part of a 'Managing Equality and Diversity Competence' programme. Personal goals and measures are to be set for individual managers as part of the programme, which will affect their performance pay. This helps ensure that a concern for diversity becomes central to how managers do their jobs and helps managers focus on developing the right skills and behaviours for successfully managing diversity in the workplace.

Similarly, at the Environment Agency[3], managers have been set recruitment targets to boost the representation of black and minority ethnic people among the workforce, and how they perform against those targets will affect their bonus payments. Rob Sutton, the diversity manager, explained that:

The aim was to get ethnic minority recruitment onto people's radars and the way to do it in this organisation was to include it in the key performance indicators because that's what managers focus on here.

As with any measures used in performance-related pay schemes, diversity measures must be carefully thought out and implemented or the wrong actions and behaviours could be encouraged. If they are not realistic and achievable, there could be a backlash against the whole diversity programme. At the Environment Agency, the targets that were set were regional rather than national, and were set for recruitment rather than for representation within the whole workforce. They therefore recognised that managers would only be able to affect what was happening in their area, and that if they had low turnover, boosting overall representation would be difficult for them to achieve. The Agency also made sure that managers were given adequate diversity skills training and guidance to help them make progress towards their targets.

Finally, a great number of diversity initiatives have relied upon the voluntary help of employees. For example, employee networks for under-represented groups, such as women, black and minority ethnic workers or gay, lesbian and bisexual employees, have, as well as providing support to those particular employees, assisted with activities such as recruitment, training design, and product development and marketing campaigns, which have had positive business returns. Organisations perhaps need to consider changing job descriptions and rewarding the individuals who volunteer to help implement such initiatives if diversity is seen not as an add-on, goodwill activity, but as a core business objective.

Recognising diversity

In organisations that are diverse, reward and diversity professionals need to work together to ensure that the reward system recognises that there is a wide range of individual lifestyle needs and motivations within the workforce. Such a system would move away from traditional 'one-size-fits-all' pay and benefits packages to allow individuals to vary reward to suit their particular needs and interests. It would include:

◘ a flexible benefits package

◘ a focus on total reward

◘ flexible working opportunities for all employees.

There would also be recognition that the most effective way of rewarding an individual may change over time as their priorities and their lifestyle changes, and that these changes may occur at different times for different individuals, so the reward package would not be fixed, and employees would have the freedom to discuss and request changes at particular intervals.

Flexible benefits

Flexible benefits schemes allow employees to select their own benefits from a range of options, beyond a mandatory or core level of benefits, or to take additional salary instead. Core benefits usually include such things as maternity provision and a minimum level of life cover and pension benefits. Usually employees re-choose or can request changes in their flexible benefits each year and many schemes also allow employees to alter their package after significant life events such as the birth of a child, marriage or divorce.

Flexible benefits and equal pay legislation

The Equal Pay Act entitles a woman (or man) to equality in each individual term of their contract with a man (or woman) doing equal work. This means comparisons are made on each individual item of reward and not on the basis of the whole remuneration package. This might raise questions about the legal justifiability of flexible benefits packages, which allow individuals to vary their terms. However, it is unlikely that an individual would claim the same level of a particular benefit with another individual, if they themselves have selected a lower level in order to have more of something else in the flexible benefits package. If the organisation makes it clear that everyone doing equal work has the same amount of money to spend on flexible benefits, the fund itself could be viewed as a single contract term. Furthermore, if a claim were brought, the existence of a flexible benefits scheme could constitute a genuine and material reason for the differences in levels of individual benefits within it.

Total reward

Total reward recognises that pay is not the only motivator and that other things such as career development opportunities, working time flexibility, and the working environment, can be equally important ways of engaging employees. Total reward is often the next logical step following the implementation of flexible benefits. While the latter caters to individual diversity in a specific part of the reward package, total reward encourages a holistic view of the entire package and how it can be customised to the individual.

> **'Total reward fits with diversity, in that its focus is on valuing employees as individuals and what they need to feel engaged.'**

Total reward fits with diversity, in that its focus is on valuing employees as individuals and what they need to feel engaged. It requires and encourages a culture in which the employee is listened to and respected, and assumptions about what motivates different kinds of individuals are avoided. Caroline Waters, Director of People Networks, BT, describes their approach:

We really do look at individuals in the round. We've got a whole piece on our intranet system aimed at managers, which talks them through how reward isn't just financial, it's much more holistic – how well do you know your person? What really turns them on? We've got lots of choices about how you do that and how you motivate them. And we never make assumptions about what individuals want. We hold regular one-to-ones with individuals and they are all based on a career life plan that encourages people to talk very openly about their own aspirations, why they want to do things and what switches them on.

Flexible working

It would be difficult to envisage a total reward approach that did not have flexible working at its heart, as the flexibility to vary working hours and/or some choice over where and when work is carried out, is becoming one of the major factors affecting individuals' choice of employer and their level of commitment at work.

Social and cultural change has led to far more dual-income and single-parent households, so the assumption that when an organisation employs someone they are getting a 'two for one' deal – someone at home taking care of all the domestic responsibilities as well as the paid employee – is unrealistic in the present day. Employers need to recognise the pressures employees are under to balance work with their domestic lives.

But flexible working is not just about parents and carers. In an organisation where flexible working is widely practised, taking time off for religious observance or prayer, or for regular medical treatment for disabled employees, will not be such an issue and these groups of employees are, therefore, less likely to be viewed as being 'difficult' and requiring some kind of 'special' treatment or accommodation. Furthermore, flexible working, if open to all, shows that the organisation values individual diversity and recognises and accepts individual differences in workstyle and productivity.

However, flexible working has proved hard for many organisations to implement. Line managers have felt that they have had to make uncomfortable judgements about individuals' lifestyles, and what are acceptable reasons for changes in working hours, and have feared or faced a backlash from employees who feel their flexibility and choice has been curtailed by other employees' working time preferences being met.

Nevertheless, if the principles and approach to implementing fair reward, which were outlined in earlier chapters, are followed when implementing flexible working, some of these dilemmas should be avoided. This means the organisation needs to:

◘ adopt and communicate a clear flexible working policy

◘ establish clear and objective business-related criteria against which individual employees' flexible working requests will be assessed

◘ give line managers adequate training and support so that they can implement the policy effectively and treat individuals in a fair and objective way

◘ monitor line-manager decisions and the effectiveness of flexible working in practice.

Endnotes

1   IDS. 'Case study: Ford's best in class maternity policy'. *IDS Diversity at Work*. No.3, September 2004. pp8–11.

2   IDS. 'Case study: London Underground improves gender balance'. *IDS Diversity at Work*. No. 4, October 2004. pp9–12.

3   IDS. 'Environment agency sets managers race targets'. *IDS Diversity at Work*. No.9, March 2005. p2.

7 | Key recommendations for action

Getting started

◘ Assess your organisation's approach to reward and diversity. If you have formal written strategies, then review them alongside each other and look for areas of overlap. Consider how they can be better aligned with each other and with the overall business strategy.

◘ Think about what the reward package says about your organisation – what assumptions have you made about the kind of people you are seeking to recruit, retain and develop? Did you consult any diversity specialists either within or outside your organisation when designing your reward system? Did you consider what impact it might have on different groups? Remember that employee engagement and motivation isn't just about the money. To build employee trust in the organisation and a willingness to work towards organisational goals, people need to see that they are treated in a fair and objective way and that includes being rewarded fairly.

◘ Think about what you know about the actual reward distribution in your organisation. It is easy to say that reward is distributed in a fair and objective way but how do you know if this really is the case? Have you checked to see if unjustified pay gaps have emerged between different groups of employees? What measures have you put in place to ensure that reward is being implemented in the way it was intended?

Auditing reward

◘ Carry out an equal pay review to find out what is happening in practice. This will alert you to any problem areas and will help you plan what action is needed to make reward fairer and to ensure more effective implementation of the reward strategy.

◘ When doing an equal pay review don't just consider whether the reward practices are compliant with the Equal Pay Act. If you find pay gaps between those doing equal work, think about whether they are justified from a business perspective as well. Do they fit with what the organisation is trying to achieve on reward and diversity?

◘ Involve both reward and diversity staff in the equal pay review. Those responsible for reward will provide insight into how the reward system has evolved and why pay gaps have arisen. Diversity specialists will help determine whether pay gaps are justifiable from an equity perspective and will shed light on other issues that might be uncovered, such as the concentration of women and ethnic minorities in particular kinds of work.

◘ Don't be put off by difficulties accessing data. Equal pay reviews should not be a one-off exercise but should be repeated at regular intervals. Initially, whatever analysis can be done should be done, and where workforce diversity or reward data is lacking, action should be planned to improve monitoring and information systems in subsequent years.

◘ Use analytical job evaluation to determine where individuals are doing equal work. This is the most rational and objective method of comparing jobs, and an equal pay review based on such a scheme will give the most reliable results.

◘ If analytical job evaluation is not possible, organisations should seek to compare the pay of those in the same grade, those with similar job titles such as 'manager' or 'team leader', and those in jobs requiring similar levels of responsibility, skill, or qualification. For further advice, see the guidance notes to the EOC's *Equal pay review kit* or, if you are a small business, see the EOC's *Equal pay, fair pay – A small business guide to effective pay practices*.

◘ If you are a large employer with numerous business units and different reward structures, consider carrying out small pilot reviews of particular areas of the business or parts of the workforce, to establish what kind of data is needed and what kind of problems might arise, before rolling the process out across the whole organisation.

◘ When comparing pay, averages are a good starting point, but remember, they hide a lot of detail. Compare medians, which strip out the influence of extreme values, and look at pay distributions, which will help you identify where individuals are earning a lot more or a lot less than is normal for a particular role.

◘ Analysis by other diversity dimensions, such as ethnicity, disability, and age, should eventually be incorporated into the review. Remember, fair reward is not just a gender issue. And, if you are a public sector organisation, there is additional legal pressure to ensure non-discrimination in reward by ethnicity or disability because of the positive duties to promote equality in these areas.

◘ Small sample sizes may make it hard to come to meaningful conclusions when comparing the average pay of ethnic minority or disabled staff. In these instances, try to match samples by identifying individuals in the majority group with similar characteristics, such as work histories, to those in the minority group.

◘ With the findings of your equal pay review, think about what you can do to make reward fairer. This is not just about compensating individuals who might have equal pay claims. Think about what you have learnt about how the reward structure and processes operate in practice and consider whether they can be improved. Can the reward structure be redesigned to prevent the risk of unjustifiable pay gaps between those doing equal work arising? Are reward decision-makers being given adequate training? Are policies on reward transparent and properly understood by employees and by those implementing them?

Ensuring fairness in reward systems

◘ Begin from the principle that all individuals, not just women compared to men, should receive equal pay for equal work.

◘ If there is an objectively justifiable business-related reason for varying pay for those doing equal work, such as to encourage higher performance or to recruit and retain in areas where there are skill or labour shortages, then clearly state the basis on which such variations will occur. Action then needs to be taken to ensure that variations only occur on that basis and that they do in fact help the organisation achieve its business objectives.

◘ Grading structures should be based upon analytical job evaluation so that the founding principle of fair reward, equal pay for equal work, is met. There is a danger that bias can be built into the job evaluation scheme itself but, to avoid this, make sure the factors against

which jobs are scored are relevant to all jobs in the organisation, that job evaluation panels are representative of the whole workforce, and that all decisions are monitored. For further guidance see the EOC's good practice guide, *Job evaluation schemes free from sex bias*.

◘ If you are a small employer and an analytical job evaluation exercise is out of the question, draw up job descriptions which systematically break down the content and demands of each job, in a way that encourages rational and objective comparisons to be made.

◘ Narrow grading structures or spot rates provide a more transparent link between job evaluation results and pay and are, therefore, more likely to ensure equal pay for equal work. However, remember that as jobs grow and change they will have to be re-evaluated and re-graded at regular intervals.

◘ Broad pay bands provide greater flexibility and can be more responsive to change, as they minimise the need for frequent re-gradings, but large pay gaps between individuals within them can more easily emerge and any justifications for them can be easily forgotten. If broad bands are used, there must be clear guidance on reward principles, reward decisions should be monitored, and records should be kept of the reasons behind pay differentials.

◘ If you have long-service-related pay scales, question the justifiability of them – does longer service always translate into greater competence and effectiveness in post? Remember, such pay scales can be discriminatory against women, who tend to accrue less service because of career breaks, and against younger workers.

◘ When designing performance-based reward systems, consult diversity specialists and ensure the criteria being adopted for assessing performance are not subjective or biased.

◘ If behaviour-based measures of performance are used, be very clear about what kind of behaviours will not be tolerated, but don't be over-prescriptive about what constitutes good behaviour. Valuing diversity means accepting there are different ways of achieving the same goals.

◘ Beware of the inherent prejudices and bias that can exist in 'market' pay rates. The case for higher pay for market reasons must be based upon up-to-date pay benchmark information, which covers the relevant geographic or occupational labour market. You should also establish that pay is, in fact, the reason why you are unable to recruit and retain staff. What do the results of exit interviews show? Are you advertising in the right place and in the right way? Are you focusing on too narrow a recruitment pool?

◘ If reward decisions are devolved to line managers, train them on how to apply the principles of diversity to reward. They must be made aware of the dangers of stereotyping and the importance of objectivity in assessing performance, for instance. And they must also be conscious of the impact their *ad hoc* decisions, on things like starting salaries and market supplements, can have on internal equity.

◘ Monitor reward decisions on an ongoing basis. Check performance appraisal ratings for evidence of bias before translating them into pay awards. Similarly, review starting salaries, market supplements, and bonus payments and keep records of the reasons for any variations from the principle of equal pay for equal work.

Communications

◘ Communicate to employees the principles on which your reward system is based and give them a basic understanding of how the reward processes work. Employees need to know at the outset what to expect, or they are likely to perceive the reward processes and outcomes as being unfair.

◘ Reward communications need to be jargon-free and in a language that employees understand. Do not just reproduce policy or strategy documents designed for reward or HR specialists.

◘ Communicate often and by every means possible. Employees need to be frequently reminded about reward objectives, how they fit with the business objectives, how the reward processes work, and how their individual reward package was determined.

◘ Being open about equal pay reviews and the findings of them can have a positive effect on employee engagement. However, if there are negative aspects to the findings, be thoughtful about what and how they are communicated. You need to communicate not just the findings but what the organisation is doing to improve the situation, and you must ensure that there is substance behind any pledges to make reward fairer or goodwill will soon turn to cynicism.

◘ If there has previously been an adversarial employment relationship, you may want to take steps to improve the employee relations climate before openly communicating the findings of equal pay reviews and openly committing to make reward fairer.

◘ Listen to what employees have to say about reward. Include questions about reward in employee opinion surveys and hold focus groups or forums to get employee feedback. Don't underestimate the extent to which employees talk about pay with each other and how concerned and upset they can become about perceived inequities.

◘ Make sure line managers are regularly updated and trained on reward issues so they can communicate effectively with employees and create realistic expectations. Line managers

need to understand the damage they can cause to morale and perceptions of fairness in the long term by making promises that are not then fulfilled.

Promoting diversity through reward

◘ Consider whether the reward package could be adapted to help the organisation attract more individuals from under-represented groups. Offering more paid and unpaid leave options, for example, might help attract and retain those with parental or caring responsibilities.

◘ Get managers to focus on diversity goals by incorporating diversity objectives and measures into their performance targets.

◘ Reward employees who take action to promote diversity in the organisation. For example, rather than relying solely on the efforts of volunteers to run employee networks for under-represented groups, incorporate such activities into the individuals' job roles and give them paid time off to carry them out.

◘ If an organisation recognises individual diversity then the reward package should not be a 'one-size-fits-all' proposition. There should be some room for the package to be tailored to meet different individual needs and motivations. This could be achieved through a total reward approach with a flexible benefits package and flexible working opportunities for all.

Further reading

ADVISORY CONCILIATION AND ARBITRATION SERVICE (2005)

Evidence to Women and Work Commission. London: Advisory Conciliation and Arbitration Service.

ADVISORY CONCILIATION AND ARBITRATION SERVICE (2004)

Pay systems. Advisory Booklet. London: Advisory Conciliation and Arbitration Service. Online version also available at: http://www.acas.org.uk/index.aspx?articleid=716.

ARMSTRONG, M. (2002)

Employee reward. 3rd ed. London: Chartered Institute of Personnel and Development.

BROWN, D. (2001)

Reward strategies: from intent to impact. London: Chartered Institute of Personnel and Development.

CHARTERED INSTITUTE OF PERSONNEL AND DEVELOPMENT (2005)

Flexible working: impact and implementation. An employer survey. London: Chartered Institute of Personnel and Development. Also available at: http://www.cipd.co.uk/surveys.

CHARTERED INSTITUTE OF PERSONNEL AND DEVELOPMENT (2005)

Flexible working: the implementation challenge. London: Chartered Institute of Personnel and Development. Also available at: http://www.cipd.co.uk/surveys.

CHARTERED INSTITUTE OF PERSONNEL AND DEVELOPMENT (2006)

Reward management: annual survey report 2006. London: Chartered Institute of Personnel and Development. Available at: http://www.cipd.co.uk/surveys.

EQUAL OPPORTUNITIES COMMISSION (2003)

Code of practice on equal pay. Manchester: Equal Opportunities Commission.

EQUAL OPPORTUNITIES COMMISSION (2003)

Equal pay, fair pay: a small business guide to effective pay practices. Manchester: Equal Opportunities Commission.

EQUAL OPPORTUNITIES COMMISSION (2003)

Equal pay review kit. Manchester: Equal Opportunities Commission.

EQUAL OPPORTUNITIES COMMISSION (2003)

Job evaluation schemes free of sex bias. Good Practice Guide. Manchester: Equal Opportunities Commission.

EQUAL PAY TASK FORCE (2001)

Just pay. Manchester: Equal Opportunities Commission.

GUEST, D.E. and CONWAY, N. (2002)

Pressure at work and the psychological contract. London: Chartered Institute of Personnel and Development.

INCOMES DATA SERVICES (2004)

'Ford's 'best in class' maternity policy'. *IDS Diversity at Work.* No 3, September. pp8–11.

INCOMES DATA SERVICES (2004)

'London Underground improves gender balance'. *IDS Diversity at Work.* No 4, October. pp8–12.

INCOMES DATA SERVICES (2005)

'Environment agency sets managers race targets'. *IDS Diversity at Work*. No 9, March. p2.

INCOMES DATA SERVICES (2005)

'Tackling equal pay at Lloyds TSB'. *IDS Diversity at Work*. No 14, August. pp8–12.

KANDOLA, R. and FULLERTON, J. (1998)

Diversity in action: managing the mosaic. 2nd ed. London: Institute of Personnel and Development.

KINGSMILL, D. (2001)

A review of women's employment and pay. London: Women and Equality Unit.

NEATHEY, F., WILLISON, R., and AKROYD, K. (2005)

Equal pay reviews in practice. Working Paper Series no.33. Manchester: Equal Opportunities Commission.

SCHÄFER, S., WINTERBOTHAM, M., and McANDREW F. (2005)

Equal pay reviews survey 2004. Working Paper Series no.32. Manchester: Equal Opportunities Commission.